Mafeking: a Diary of a Siege

WRECKING THE ARMOURED TRAIN AT KRAAIPAN

Mafeking: a Diary of a Siege

A Classic Account of a Famous Engagement
of the Boer War

F. D. Baillie

LEONAUR

Mafeking: a Diary of a Siege
A Classic Account of a Famous Engagement of the Boer War
by F. D. Baillie

First published under the title
Mafeking: a Diary of a Siege

Leonaur is an imprint of Oakpast Ltd

Copyright in this form © 2013 Oakpast Ltd

ISBN: 978-1-78282-062-8 (hardcover)
ISBN: 978-1-78282-063-5 (softcover)

http://www.leonaur.com

Contents

Prefatory Note   7

The Siege of Mafeking   9

Prefatory Note

I must crave the indulgence of the public for producing a more or less rough form of diary in the form of a book, and it is only the interest which they have manifested in Mafeking which has induced me to do so. To the proprietor of *The Morning Post* I am indebted for his kindness in allowing me to republish the diary in book form. To the proprietors of *The Daily Graphic* I am indeed grateful for the sketches with which they have allowed me to supplement my diary. Such as it is, I dedicate it to all members of my dear old regiment, past and present. Four of us were serving there: myself, and Private Brierly, B squadron, now B.S.A.P., Private Williams and Private Lambart, D squadron (the former now sergeant), Protectorate Regiment, while the adjutant of the I.L.H. portion of the relieving force was Captain Barnes, also B squadron. These are only matters of regimental interest, but as the publication is dedicated to the regiment, I feel justified in giving these details.

F. D. Baillie, Major,
late 4th Queen's Own Hussars.

SIGNALLING FROM AN ARMOURED TRAIN.

The Siege of Mafeking

War declared tonight, October 10th, 1899, by old Kruger. So much the better, this intolerable waiting is over.

This I find is the entry in my diary for that date, but little did I know we were about to commence the "Siege of Mafeking"—a much more intolerable wait, with the additional pleasure of being fired at without the chance of returning it with effect.

Till you have experienced it no one (at least I hadn't) has any idea how trying it is to exist without news of the outside world.

On October 11th nothing happened. On the 12th, the Protectorate Regiment under Colonel Hore took up a position on the eastern heights, which overlook the town and waited attack. The Boers, however, did not arrive.

In the meantime the town defences under Colonel Vyvyan and Major Panzera were progressing apace. We had only quite recently been enabled to do anything in that direction, owing to the repressive policy of the Bond Ministry. Therefore the defences at this time consisted merely of a few breastworks, wagons drawn across the ends of roads leading on to the market square, and a few strands of barbed wire fastened up on these points.

October 13th, 1899. In the morning the same programme; the Boers reported to the south and also to the north. Whilst lying on the heights—if they can be so called—we saw a magnificent sight. For safety two trucks of dynamite were being run up to a northern siding clear of the town. About eight miles out the Boers commenced firing. The engine-driver uncoupled his trucks and ran his engine back towards the town. The Boers closed in and continued firing, thinking it was the armoured train. Result—a terrific explosion, a column of smoke shooting up into the air and mushrooming out until it became a vast cloud in the clear blue sky. In the afternoon I went out in the armoured train to inspect the damage, but they had pulled up the line short of the spot. We opened with a Maxim on the body of Boers engaged in inspecting the hole and bagged a couple. The remainder galloped in the utmost confusion towards their *laager*.

The armoured train had previously been out in the morning due south and bagged one, and went out again in the same direction on its return, under Captain Williams, and secured another.

October 14th, 1899. The fight today may be summarized thus: Boers firing on the picquets; Boer retirement harassed by the armoured train, which was eventually supported by one squadron, which engaged the retreating Boers heavily. The Boers tried to cut them off, but the arrival of another squadron and a seven-pounder settled the matter. Their attack was repelled with great loss, and we retired to our lines.

Whilst we were at breakfast firing was heard in the direction of the cemetery to the north of the town, and shortly afterwards increased in volume; then came the bark of the Maxim, the boom of heavy guns and the increasing rattle of musketry. D squadron of the Protectorate Regiment was ordered out to support the armoured train. We waited on the Market Square knowing nothing, hearing only the heavy fire.

What had transpired was this: a squadron of the Protectorate Regiment commanded by Lord Charles Bentinck had furnished a strong patrol to discover the whereabouts of the Boers. He happened to come upon them about four miles out. They promptly pursued and tried to cut him off. The corporal with his right flank patrol galloped on to the armoured train, and on his own initiative directed it to move out in support. The Boers were driven back, hotly engaged by the armoured train, in charge of Captain Williams, British South Africa Police, a train which was constructed and conducted by Lieutenant More, Railway Volunteers. The train drove their artillery from two positions; their shells burst all round, under and over the train, and, strange to say, only two men were slightly scratched.

At that period Captain Fitzclarence arrived, and engaged the Boers who were withdrawing, firing at the armoured train, towards their own *laager*. To explain the situation now, I must describe the field of battle. The railway runs due north and south of Mafeking. The Boers' laager about eight miles N.N.E. of the town. The train had driven the enemy about five miles and a half back from the town, therefore

The Crew of the H.M.S. "Firefly."

by this divergence, when Captain Fitzclarence came into action he had perforce lost the effective support of the train, and the squadron fought on its own account. It numbered about seventy men: it faced about five or six hundred. Two orderlies were sent to Captain Fitzclarence and the armoured train to tell them to fall back, one on a bicycle who was captured, and the other on horseback.

Now to show the advantage of khaki as a fighting colour on the well-bleached *veldt*. The horseman rode up to the Boers and was fired upon. He then galloped along the front of, and through and along the rear of our own men without seeing a man, delivered his message to the armoured train, and returned to seek his invisible friends unsuccessfully. His horse was shot, and he returned to Mafeking on an engine. In at least two instances he was within thirty yards of his own men and could not see them. The dark clothing of the Boers is, however, more conspicuous, but with smokeless powder and khaki the firing line even at short ranges is invisible as a target.

To return to the actual fight. The Boers pelted by a well-directed fire returned a wild and ineffectual one. The incidents of the fight commenced. Two cousins, Corporals Walshe and Parland, Irishmen, and men of means who had joined not for pay but for patriotism, quickly fell, both shot through the head by the same Dutchman, who was ensconced in a tree, but unfortunately for himself he let fall a piece of paper which caught the quick eye of Private Wormald, who promptly picked him off like a rook. Several other Dutchmen in like positions met the same fate. This treatment did not appeal to the Boer, who came out to shoot and not to be shot at, and so he made his usual move to work round and cut off the squadron from their base.

At the distance the squadron was from the line (over three quarters of a mile), and at the angle it was to the line, in addition to the difficulty with smokeless powder of telling friend from foe, it was impossible for the armoured train to act. Previous to this they had been supported by a troop of A squadron under Lieutenant Brady who was wounded on coming into action. The situation was distinctly serious, their flank was nearly turned, and the Boers had almost interposed themselves between the squadron and Mafeking; at this critical juncture Lord Charles Bentinck and two more troops with a seven-pound gun arrived within striking distance. Two rounds of shrapnel and the Boers commenced retiring. When their retirement was assured D squadron withdrew, placing their wounded in the armoured train. The fight was over.

Surgeon-Major Anderson, who had had his horse shot, attended to the wounded throughout the fight in the firing line. Our losses were two killed, twelve wounded, two of whom subsequently died. Four horses killed, twelve wounded. Boer losses reported eighty killed, about twice that number wounded.

Too much credit cannot be given to Captain Fitzclarence and Lord Charles Bentinck for the coolness and gallantry with which they handled their men, or to the men for the way they responded, and what is said of them applies in the same degree to Captain Williams and the men of the British South Africa Police and Railway Volunteers engaged. The Boers had fought in the scrub, in vastly superior numbers and had been thoroughly beaten.

The strain on Colonel Baden-Powell and the headquarter staff must indeed have been great. For four hours they were anxiously waiting, reports were not favourable, and they knew that a disaster to a small force engaged risked the whole defence as there was literally not another man to send to their support. Indeed one squadron engaged was actually a part of the defence of the northern portion of the town. On the return of the wounded a train with a relief party under Major Baillie with Father Ogle, and Mr. Peart, Wesleyan minister, went to recover the bodies, and if necessary to render assistance to any wounded Boers who might have been left in the retreat. The train stopped near the scene of the action and the party with stretchers, preceded by a large Red Cross flag, moved towards the spot. They were fired on about half a mile before they reached it, and as the firing increased it was decided to retire as the men were known to be dead, and all the wounded were brought in.

This they did quietly, the Boers in the meantime were working round to the line to cut them off from the train. The train returned to Mafeking, and on a report being made to Colonel Baden-Powell he addressed a letter of remonstrance to General Cronje.

15th, Sunday. Landau and pair, with huge Red Cross flag, arrived containing Dr. Pirow, Cronje's doctor, who came to lunch. He explained that the firing on the Red Cross was a mistake, as the Boers thought that the train was the armoured train returning, and gave us news of Lieutenant Nesbitt and our prisoners of the armoured train which has been captured at Kraaipan. He took whisky and beer back with him for Cronje. Sunday is a tacit truce with both parties, and no fighting goes on. I suppose we are the only two nations who would observe it. The ambulance went out and fetched in the dead. They were buried by moonlight by Father Ogle, a most impressive ceremony. The Father said a few words to the effect that it was a righteous war, and that the Sisters were praying for us.

16th, Monday. The Boers brought up two twelve-pounders to a long-range position N.-E. of the town and commenced bombarding. They drove in our picquet at the head of the waterworks and occupied the trench. They directed their fire mainly on the town and station, consequently did most damage in the convent, which was flying the Red Cross and was fitted up as a hospital. The shells that missed the convent struck the centre of the town, but did little harm. The shells that missed the station pitched round the B.S.A.P. fort, which was occupied by Colonel Hore and a squadron of the Protectorate Regiment. This they continued all day. Casualties *nil.* Our seven-pounders out-ranged. No reply made to their fire.

The Boers had thus occupied the head of the waterworks and cut off our water supply. The headquarter staff had made provision for this, and under Major Hepworth's supervision had had all wells cleaned out and Sir Charles Warren's old well reopened. We thus have an abundance of water.

Towards mid-day a flag of truce, borne by a renegade English Colonial, rode towards our lines. This was unfortunate. They had not detected the armoured train, and the skirmishing line of the Boers and their artillery was just coming within deadly Maxim range. They rode straight on to the armoured train, and of course the trap was disclosed. It was a message from Cronje, who sent in to demand surrender to avoid further bloodshed. Baden-Powell answered, "Certainly, but when will bloodshed begin?" and pointed out that they were again firing on the Red Cross flag.

Two of our wounded, both corporals, died today. The town is practically surrounded.

17th, 18th, and 19th. Nothing happened. Investment completed. Boers estimated six thousand men, undoubtedly correct.

20th. Boers cut off some cattle which had strayed out too far.

21st. In addition to the main railway line, a temporary line had been laid down in an easterly direction towards the race course, and north of the town extending about a mile and a half. The armoured train now patrolled this line; painted green and covered with bushes,

FIRING FROM AN ARMOURED TRAIN

it was indistinguishable from the scrub surrounding it. I slept in the armoured train at the railhead. In the early morning Captain Williams commenced firing on the Boers at the head of the waterworks as they came out of their trench to make their coffee, with two Maxims. I fear they got their coffee rather late, and that some even did not get it at all. This went on with fitful replies for two or three hours, and then firing in that quarter ceased.

On the western front in the afternoon the Boers looted some cattle which had strayed, and from this date sniping commenced, pretty generally all round on both sides.

22nd, Sunday. Band and calls on various outlying forts, hospitals, &c. All church services were held.

And now to endeavour to describe the town and defences of Mafeking. Mafeking is situated on a rise about three hundred yards north of the Molopo River, which flows from east to west. It is about three-quarters of a mile square. The railroad runs to the west of the town, and practically speaking, due north and south, but immediately south where it crosses the Molopo by an iron bridge it inclines rather westward for a distance of two or three miles. The railway embankment north and south of the river thus furnishes cover from the east and south-east heights on the southern bank of the Molopo.

To the west again of the railway, and nearly butting it half a mile south of the Molopo, is the native *stadt*, lying on both sides of the river, and on the northern bank, commencing about half a mile from the railway, then running in a north-westerly direction for about a mile and a half, and ends about a mile and three-quarters west of the railway. The ground in front of the northern end is slightly higher than the *stadt* and soon commences to sink away from it, affording good cover to an enemy moving on that side. Near the railway the ground slopes gradually down for a considerable distance to the river. The country round Mafeking to the west, north and east, is flat, but across the Molopo to the south and south east it commands the town. The ground to the west of the *stadt* commands the *stadt*.

Situated two thousand yards south, and slightly east of the centre of the town, is an old fort of Sir Charles Warren's—Cannon Kopje. This is the key of the position. It is an old circular stone fort, and only by dint of extraordinary exertion had it been possible to bring it by this time up in any degree to a state of efficiency enough to enable it to resist even old ordinary seven-pounder guns. It has an interior diameter of approximately twenty-five yards. The native location occupied by half-breeds lies directly between Cannon Kopje and the town on the southern bank of the river. Following the course of the river eastward about twelve hundred yards from the town, and on the northern bank extend the brickfields (eventually occupied by both parties), while in the same direction, and about three miles and a half from Mafeking on a ridge, is MacMullan's farm (subsequently the Boer headquarters). To return to the town—at the north-eastern corner is the convent. Due east of that is the grand stand about a mile away, while N.N.E. from the convent, and a mile and a half away, is the base of the waterworks, which extend to a trench at their head in the same direction for nearly a mile.

Thus we have the railway station the north-west corner, the convent the north-east corner, Ellis's house the south-east corner, and the south-west corner the pound; while in a line from the south-west corner of the town and the northern portion of the *stadt*, the B.S.A.P. barracks and fort lie about midway. With the exception of a strip of scrub about a mile wide to the north and east of the convent the country all round is almost bare.

The town is composed of one-storey houses built of soft bricks and roofed with corrugated iron, the only exception being the convent of two storeys and the station, which is not yet complete. The native *stadt* consists of *kaffir* huts. The B.S.A.P. fort is a duplicate of Cannon Kopje, thus the outline of the defences of Mafeking is, roughly speaking, an obtuse angled triangle, of which the apex is Cannon Kopje, while the other two angles are the northern end of the native *stadt* and the convent. The population in time of peace is, Mafeking two thousand whites, the native *stadt* four to five thousand, location five hundred. At the present moment fifteen hundred whites approximately, native *stadt* seven thousand owing to native refugees, location five hundred.

The perimeter of the defences was between five and six miles. Commencing with the convent, and working westward at the outset, the defences were as follows:—The railway line and armoured train protected the north-west front, then nearer to the railway came Fort Victoria, occupied by Railway Volunteers; and in the arc of a circle extending to the north end of the *stadt* trenches occupied by the Protectorate Regiment at night. These were gradually turned into forts. The women's *laager* was established on the edge of the *stadt* near the B.S.A.P. officers' quarters, and a refugee camp in the hollow north of the *stadt*, the northern end of which was held by Captain Vernon and

C squadron Protectorate Regiment, while B squadron, under Captain Marsh, and the natives, held the *stadt* itself—the whole under Major Godley, who commanded the western outposts. The town was garrisoned by the Cape Police under Captains Brown and Marsh; these and the Railway Volunteers being under Colonel Vyvyan, while Cannon Kopje was entrusted to Colonel Walford and the B.S.A.P. Colonel Baden-Powell retained one squadron of the Protectorate Regiment as reserve under his own immediate control.

These arrangements were subsequently much augmented. After the convent had been practically demolished by shell fire and the railway line all round the town pulled up or mined during the close investment by the Boers, the small work was erected at the convent corner, garrisoned by the Cape Police and a Maxim, under Lieutenant Murray, who was also put in charge of the armoured train, which had, however, been withdrawn to the railway station out of harm's way. The Railway Volunteers garrisoned the cemetery, and had an advanced trench about eight hundred yards to the front and immediately to the right of the line. To the westward came Fort Cardigan, and then again Fort Miller. In the south-west was Major Godley's fort, at the north of the native *stadt*, with an advance fort—Fort Ayr—crowning the down to the northern end of the *stadt*. Although this was rather detached, it commanded a view and fire for a great distance to the south of the northern portion of the *stadt*, and here the Cape Police were entrenched with the Maxim.

Five hundred yards to the west front of Captain Marsh's post lay Limestone Fort, commanding the valley, on the other side of which lay the Boer *laager* and entrenchments. At the south-western corner, and on the edge of the *stadt* Captain Marsh's fort was situated. The whole of the edge of the *stadt* was furnished with loopholes and trenches, and garrisoned by the native inhabitants. By the railway were situated two armoured trucks with a Nordenfeldt. Cannon Kopje, with two Maxims and a seven-pounder, lay to the south-east. And now to the immediate defence of the town. At the south-western corner is the pound, garrisoned by Cape Police, under Captain Marsh; then eastwards Early's fort, Dixon's redan, Dall's fort, Ellis's corner, with Maxim and Cape Police, under Captain Brown.

On the eastern front, Ellitson's *kraal*, Musson's fort, De Kock's fort, with Maxim, recreation ground fort, and so back to the convent, on the left of which lies the hospital fort—all these, unless otherwise mentioned, garrisoned by Town Guard. These so-called forts are garrisoned with from fifteen to forty men, and furnished with head cover and bomb proofs against artillery. Bomb proofs have been constructed everywhere, traverses erected at the end of streets, trenches giving cover leading from every portion of the town and defences; and it is possible to walk round the town without being exposed to aimed fire. The trenches are constructed with a view to being manned in case of need. Telephones are established in all the headquarter bomb proofs of outlying forts, and are connected with the headquarter bomb proof, thus securing instant communication and avoiding the chance of orderlies being sniped, which would assuredly otherwise be the case. These defences were all improvised on the spot—every conceivable sort of material being utilized therein.

23rd, Monday. Bombardment threatened, so commenced by forestalling it. Two guns under Captain Williams, B.S.A.P., and Lieutenant Murchison, Protectorate Regiment, started at 3 a.m., to take up a position at our end of the waterworks and the rail head temporary line, respectively, with orders not to fire unless fired on. I rode out with them and saw as pretty an artillery duel in miniature as one would wish to see. We waited patiently, Lieutenant Murchison laid his gun on the enemy's seven-pounder, which we could distinctly see in their trenches at the head of the waterworks. We were under cover from view. At last a puff of smoke came from their gun, and before it was well clear of the muzzle ours had answered, and that gun was out of action for a considerable period. In the meantime, both of our guns were playing gaily on their trenches and remaining gun.

This went on intermittently till mid-day, and then both their guns ceased fire altogether. We then returned, and since heard that their guns were rendered useless for some time. On the south-western portion of the defences a similar seven-pounder fight was going on, and the Boers then fired their twelve-pounder high velocity gun a few times. Their ninety-four-pounder Creechy (an abbreviation for Marguerite) or, as the men call her, Creaky, has arrived and taken up a position at Jackall Tree, 3400 yards S.S.W. of Cannon Kopje, accompanied by some field guns.

24th. Creaky commenced her ministrations by firing about forty shells and damaged property but hurt no one. The convent of course was hit, and the twelve-pounders also joined in the fire. Marvellous escapes reported all round.

25th. Creaky began in real earnest, and also seven-pounders, twelve-pounders, Maxims, and all. They fired about four hundred shells, mostly in the direction of the convent hospital, trying, I fancy, to hit the station. I was in the trenches in the recreation ground. The convent was struck several times. Their shell fire seemed very noisy, but its effect was more moral than physical, as casualties therefrom were few; the musketry fire, however, did more damage.

The advance party down the Malmani road had a man hit badly (since dead), young Kelly, Protectorate Regiment, and when a party went out to fetch him, though obviously wounded, they were exposed to a hail of bullets—for at least half a mile. I saw the lad in the hospital, and his only anxiety was to get out and have another go at them. At the same time on the other flank the Boers made an attack on the native staff, hoping on the assurance of the Baralongs to obtain a footing there; and then when they had got us thoroughly engaged on the south-western face, their real attack was to have been made from the north. The Baralongs, however, supplemented by two squadrons of ours, greeted them with a heavy fire, killing many. Consequently that attack on our face never came off.

27th. Shelling continued, and now, having beaten the enemy in the field, Colonel Baden-Powell resolved to give them a taste of cold steel, accordingly, at 8 p.m. D squadron, fifty-three strong, paraded under Captain Fitzclarence, with two parties of the Cape Police in support. It was a fine dark night, and the squadron moved off with injunctions only to use the bayonet. The two parties of Cape Police moved towards the brickfields, one considerably further east than the other to enfilade the rear of the Boer trenches. The object of the attack was some trenches of Commandant Louw's on our side of the racecourse and to the north of the Malmani road (which runs due east of the town to Malmani). It was a still night, and lying waiting one could hear the order to charge, and then the din began. The first trench was carried with a rush; the Boers lying under tarpaulins did not hear the advance till they were almost on them

Sword and bayonet did their work well, and with the flanking parties firing on the rear trench, and the Boers commencing a heavy fire in all directions and from all quarters, things for a time were very lively indeed. It was estimated that six hundred Boers were in *laager*, so after giving them a thorough dose of the bayonet, the signal to retire was given by a loud whistle, and carried out in the same cool and orderly manner as the advance. In the meantime a furious fire was being maintained by the Boers all round; the volleys from the Cape Police completed their confusion, and they kept on firing even after the wounded had been dressed and placed in hospital. Something frightened them again about 2 a.m., and they recommenced their fusillade at nothing and continued it for about an hour.

Our losses were six killed, eleven wounded and two prisoners, including Captain Fitzclarence and Lieutenant Swinburne slightly wounded. We subsequently heard that the Boers lost one hundred—forty killed by the bayonet, and sixty whom they had probably shot themselves in the hideous confusion that reigned in their camp. Captain Fitzclarence used his sword with good effect. The Cape Police, who were under Lieutenant Murray, lost none. The attacking squadron did not fire a shot, but in the rush to the second trench the occupants probably shot their own men in the dark at close range. This story later shows the terror the Boers here have of cold steel. Our snipers were now close to the enemy's trench, and one of the Boers, probably an artilleryman, waved his sword over the top, whereupon one of his comrades was overheard to shout, "For God's sake do not do that, or they will come with their bayonets."

What I said about coolness and gallantry in the first fight applies in even a greater degree to this encounter. The men were admirably led and did splendidly. Our success so far was marked. The Boers had been kept at a respectful distance from the town. They never felt safe at night; they had been beaten at their own game in the open, and we practically disregarded their vaunted artillery, on which they had pinned their faith to reduce the town. Daily the situation became more a question of endurance.

28th. Ambulance, under a flag of truce, fetched in our dead. Boers very surly. The dead were buried that night. Shell-fire and sniping continued; little harm done.

29th, Sunday. Band, &c.

30th. Transferred my residence to the western portion to watch the Boers moving to and fro on our western front, about two miles out, sniping going on both sides all round. Desultory shell fire.

31st. Enemy's force occupied a position on the south-eastern heights and from Jackall Tree three thousand four hundred yards S.S.W. of Cannon Kopje, where they had erected earthworks, their artillery pushed forward to within two thousand yards, and opened a heavy

FITZCLARENCE'S BAYONET CHARGE.

fire on the *kopje*, commencing at 4.40 a.m., under cover of which their infantry attack was pushed from the south-east to within three hundred yards of the *kopje*, but was repelled by the B.S.A.P., fifty-seven strong, with two Maxims and a seven-pounder under Colonel Walford. They attacked with great resolution, but our fire was held till they came within good range, and then after sustaining it for some time they broke and fled. Their ambulances came to pick up the dead and, under their cover, many who had been playing "possum" got up and ran for their lives.

Our losses were six killed, including Captain the Hon. D. H. Marsham and Captain Pechell, K.R.R., and two sergeant-majors, five wounded severely. I may perhaps be permitted to say a few words about personal friends. It seemed as if it could not be true. In Captain Marsham's case, well known as he was to the Boers, and popular as he was on both sides of the border, the enemy will regret his death almost as deeply as his comrades here did. Captain Pechell had a brother serving here as a private in the Protectorate, who has since got his commission in that regiment; an additional sympathy must be felt for his family and regiment, as almost at the same time his brother in the same regiment was killed in a Natal fight. I only voice the one feeling here of personal sorrow for their loss and sympathy with their relations.

The Boers were well thrashed, and my previous description of Cannon Kopje will enable readers to grasp what a thoroughly gallant fight it was. The Boers must have lost very heavily. Later in the day they attacked the southern end of the native *stadt*, in a half-hearted manner, but it was not pushed home, and were easily driven off. Both these fights were easily visible across the valley, with the exception of the commencement of the Boer infantry advance, which one could only gather from the continuous musketry fire. This night we buried the dead, all the available officers in the garrison attending.

November 1st. The enemy shelled Cannon Kopje again, and galloped up from the south within about a mile, dismounted, and made a show of attack, but were driven away. Shell fire and sniping.

2nd. Desultory shell fire and lots of sniping at horses watering, five horses wounded. At about 10 p.m. Lieutenant Murchison shot Mr. Parslow, *Daily Chronicle* representative, but as the matter is still *sub judice*, comments or opinions are undesirable.

3rd. Heavy shelling and sniping. The Boers having occupied a position in the brickfields, Captain Goodyear and the Cape Boys attacked them and turned them out, during which Captain Goodyear was unfortunately severely wounded in the leg.

Inquest this morning returned a verdict of wilful murder against Lieutenant Murchison, who will be tried by Field General Court Martial. Mr. Parslow's funeral took place tonight, attended by the staff and many others; the other correspondents and myself carried the coffin to the grave.

4th. Heavy shelling and sniping all round, eight horses shot. The Boers having experienced the delights of the dynamite explosion, now determine to repay us in our own coin. Loading a truck with dynamite, they brought it up to the top of the incline on the railway, which runs from the north down to Mafeking Station, meaning to run it into the station and explode it in the town. In this amiable intention they were foiled, as either owing to the rustiness or roughness of the line, which had not been used for three weeks, to the defective fuse, or some other unexplained cause, it blew up a mile and a half out of town, and I trust assisted a few of them to the other world. The curious part of the explosion was that everyone insisted that a shell had burst exactly over the spot he happened to be in, and it was not until next day that the occurrence was explained.

5th. Sunday. Band, and celebrated Guy Fawkes day with fireworks, first warning the enemy not to be alarmed.

6th. A smart bit of work on the part of the Boers. Their big gun opened fire at 4.30 a.m., and after firing one shot they took her round to the south-eastern heights, where they had erected a work for her, and fired again within twelve hours; by the remote road they preferred, it must have been more than four miles; two field guns and a large escort accompanied her.

7th. Rumours were rife as to the intended attack on the native *stadt* this morning, but this pleasant attention was anticipated. At 3 a.m. Major Godley paraded with Captain Vernon's squadron, Protectorate Regiment and mounted Bechuanaland Rifles under Captain Cowan, with two seven-pounders and the Hotchkiss gun, under Lieutenant Daniel, B.S.A.P., Captain Marsh's Squadron P.R., being held in readiness to support, if necessary, from the southern portion of the *stadt*. And here it must be explained that due west the Boers had established a *laager* with about two hundred and fifty men, two twelve-pound-

Siege of Masfcking 1899

Portions of shells, fired by Boers into Woman's (Oct) Laager (Nov)

RELICS.

ers and a diabolical one-pound Maxim in entrenchments, and daily shelled the *stadt* and western defences, and that it was from this quarter that the attack was expected.

However, Major Godley took up a position within good range of the *laager*, and as day broke the Boers were roused by the seven-pounders and the Hotchkiss, supplemented by long range volleys. The Boers broke toward Cronje's large *laager*, about three or four miles south-west of the *stadt*. I was watching operations from the top of the B.S.A.P. fort, and the whole fight was clearly discernible in its earlier stages, an admirable example of Boer tactics, as their advance to their attacking position was across our western front, though at safe distance from rifle fire. Within ten minutes of the commencement of fire knots of Boers came galloping from the large *laager*, in tens, twenties, twos and threes, anyhow, in fact, and about half way they met the Boers who were retreating, who then rallied and returned with them to the attack. They swept over the ridge towards the north, and as they drew nearer were assailed by long range volleys from Captain Marsh, and then the fight began. There could not have been less than five hundred, personally I fancy eight.

Their guns were in full swing and firing wildly fortunately, for the majority of the shells burst by the women's *laager* and the fort, which did not seem logical, as we were not hurting them. Their one-pound Maxim, however, was putting in good work. The object of the sortie had been attained in drawing the attack where we wanted it, and a gradual and slow retirement on the works commenced. Then, unfortunately, one of our guns was temporarily disabled, but under a very heavy fire was righted without any casualty, which was miraculous, as the one-pounder had got the range and put shells around it all the time, shooting off the heel of a man's boot and bursting all around and among the men and horses. However, all got under cover all right. Captain Vernon handled his men coolly and well, and retiring by alternate troops they kept the enemy at bay. The fire was very heavy, and but that the majority of the Boer firing was wild, we should have lost heavily. Major Godley was shot through the hat, slightly wounded in the hand, and his horse shot.

The Bechuanaland Rifles at their baptism of fire behaved steadily and well, and Captain Cowan was well justified at his pride in his men. The Boers attacked the entrenchments, advancing to within six hundred yards of them, but were beaten off with loss. Working round to the northern flank, however, they managed to account for eleven horses and two men in about as many seconds, but the undesirable attention of the stationary Maxim convinced them that their presence was no longer necessary. It was very hot whilst it lasted, and then to the looker-on came the welcome sight of first one, then twos and threes, then larger bodies, cantering off in the direction from which they had come, and then, the most welcome sight of all, three large wagons flying the Red Cross flag coming to pick up their casualties, showing that their loss must have been heavy. Our loss, six men wounded, six horses killed, nine wounded, and many cattle and donkeys in the vicinity of the forts killed and wounded.

8th. Sniping and shelling and a new earthwork being constructed by the Boers three thousand yards due north of the B.S.A.P. Fort, called Game Tree Fort.

9th. The cheering news from Natal of three British victories has arrived, great excitement prevails, and naturally—it is our first news for nearly a month. Shelling and sniping of course goes on, and one shell burst in Colonel Walford's stable, where three horses were together, and killed the centre horse, thirty-one shrapnel bullets being found in it. The others were untouched, as were also the men all round.

10th. Game Tree fort has begun with high velocity twelve-pounders. These are pernicious guns. Old Creaky can be provided for. She is carefully watched from everywhere—if she is pointed a bell rings, when the smoke comes from her muzzle another bell rings, and everybody goes to ground till the shell does (or does not) burst. But these smokeless guns give no warning; the report and the shell arrive simultaneously. Twenty-seven shells were fired in a very short time round the fort, three burst in it, and one knocked a bucket from a nigger. But when they had got the range accurately the Boers desisted. Their artillery tactics are marvellous. They fire in a casual way at anything; if they get the range accurately they seem satisfied, and begin to shoot at something else. They keep on shooting for some time and unexpectedly stop; then just as vaguely begin again, with apparently no ulterior object, but general annoyance. One thing only is certain, that from 4.30 to 5 a.m. Creaky will fire a round or two, and probably stop till after breakfast, and that from 8.30 to 9 p.m. she has never missed her farewell shot.

11th. Shelling all day, sniping getting really lively.

12th. News of Colonel Plumer's column. We were all grieved to hear of poor Blackburne's death.

13th. Slight shell fire, very quiet all round.

14th. Sniping and shelling rather lively, to compensate for yesterday.

*15th.*Very quiet. Heavy rain during the night; the Boers entrenching themselves towards the brickfields. An American despatch rider of Reuter's, Mr. Pearson, arrived, having ridden from south of Kimberley—a great performance.

16th. Heavy thunderstorm and rain; shelling and sniping all round.

17th. Shelling and sniping. The big gun again shifted rather farther back. Mr. Pearson started on his adventurous ride back to Cape Town. I wish him every success.

18th. Today is the beginning of the end, I hope. Cronje's *laager* to the south-west is breaking up and trekking south. All squadrons have been warned to be in readiness to start at once, and we hope our turn is coming at last, but General Cronje is capable of any ruse to draw us out and endeavour to overwhelm us in the open. They do not forget to leave us Creaky, who gave us a heavy doing today; sniping is going on continually daily on our south-eastern and eastern front.

At this point of the siege it is worthwhile to review the situation. The Boers have been compelled to detach a large portion of their force to the south, leaving, however, ample men to invest the town. They have had four severe lessons and seem more disinclined than ever to come to close quarters. They have, however, entrenched themselves in suitable positions round the town, and it is impossible to say at any given point what their strength might be. Our strength is about nine hundred rifles, including all available white men, and a sortie, even if successful, might seriously impair our strength; whereas, as we are, we can hold the town, which is our primary object.

For a sortie at the most we could only hope for two hundred to two hundred and fifty men, and the rapidity with which the Boers concentrate, and their vast superiority in artillery, would give them a very good chance of inflicting a defeat, which might be ruinous. No! their shell and musketry fire is annoying, but with the precautions that have been taken they cannot inflict sufficient damage to compel surrender. Thus, the whole thing resolves itself into a matter of "patience, our turn is coming soon." For if we cannot get out, neither they nor three times their number can get in.

From this time on till the beginning of December it may be as well to explain the situation in advance. The fighting on the western and southern fronts had almost ceased, but the Boer entrenchments were occupied by picquets, who indulged in occasional sniping, and it was unknown how many were in the rear of them. The fort to the north, Game Tree Fort, was armed with a five-pounder gun, and was occupied fairly strongly, and between that and the waterworks was another trench, occupied by the Boers, from which they were eventually ousted by the fire of the Bechuanaland Rifles. To our eastern front lay the trench by the race-course, strongly held; and south of that in front of McMullen's farm (the Boer main *laager*), a trench about thirteen hundred yards from the town.

There are four or five brick-kilns about eleven to twelve hundred yards from the town, running in a diagonal direction from the trench down towards the Molopo, and it was about here that the continuous skirmishing took place; our works being pushed out to meet theirs from the bed of the river, which was connected with the town by a trench running due south from Ellis's corner, past the old Dutch church. Their guns were admirably placed for raking the town, *stadt*, and defences on the south-eastern heights, about three thousand yards from the town. To the south of the river the Cape boys occupied a trench, near the eastern end of location, and about two thousand yards from the enemy's big gun.

19th, Sunday. Band and calls. *Laager*, to the north-east at Signal Hill, trekking eastward.

20th to 23rd. Daily shelling and sniping. Captain Sandford moved the Boers and the seven-pounders from the western entrenchments. One of these guns they now abandoned with the exception of a picquet.

24th. Shelling and sniping; the B.S.A.P. Fort came in for most of it; two men wounded.

26th, Sunday. We had our first game of polo, a concert, and a football match. Church in the evening.

27th. An advanced trench had been constructed in the river bed, six hundred yards from the Boer trench, and fourteen hundred yards from the big gun: Lord Charles Bentinck occupied it after dark.

28th. The big gun was harassed by volleys all day, and did not fire much, a lively skirmish going on at intervals throughout the day on the eastern front, Maxims, guns and rifles; Cape Boys partaking from the south of the Molopo. Fitzclarence relieved Lord Charles Bentinck this evening. The Boers vacated the brick-kilns after the firing had been going on for some time.

29th. The long-range volleys have undoubtedly had good effect. The big gun cocked up her nose and fired two rounds wildly this morning. On the eastern front was a crowd with telescopes and field glasses, laughing at the gunners, who could plainly be seen dodging about, and making many futile efforts to get off their piece safely somehow. Ellis's corner, Fitzclarence's squadron, the Cape Boys in the river bed and in the trench, volleyed him directly old Creaky's muzzle was elevated. The enemy could not find out where the fire came from, and fired their smaller guns and one-pound Maxim, on chance, all about the place, but did no harm. Creaky only got off three rounds today. When the Boers in the trench tried to join in, the Maxim at Ellis's corner was turned on to them; while the Maxim from De Kock's fort paid a similar attention to the race-course trenches. The Boers in the north-west also shelled today. Lord Charles Bentinck relieved Fitzclarence after dark.

30th. This was the hottest day's firing we have had for some time. At 3 a.m. a heavy fire commenced all round. The Boers had been annoyed by our native snipers in the river and brickfields, and commenced firing so-called volleys from their trench in the direction of the river bed. The Cape Boys and the squadron fired on the big gun and Ellis's corner fired on the Boers. Our Hotchkiss also fired, but the seven-pounder gun, concealed in the bed of the river, did not fire, but awaited developments, as its position was still unknown to the enemy; this went on with short intervals all day, but an hour and an half before sundown began a most furious fusillade all round. Creaky, who had now been furnished with cover for her gunners, joined in the fray, and for over an hour heavy firing was incessant, and a very pretty fight followed.

In all this firing on the south-eastern corner the bullets drop in the town, and the market square and surrounding streets are no places for a contemplative stroll at these times. The other day, during a game of football, a ninety-four-pound shell passed through the players and burst in the town house, in the centre of the square, but marvellous to relate, none were injured though the interior of the town house has disappeared. To return to the skirmish, after a vast expenditure of ammunition our casualties were nil; I trust the enemy's were heavy. In a Transvaal paper, dated December 2nd, they confessed to several being slightly wounded lately by our continuous fire.

December 1st. To check an undesirable expenditure of ammunition, Colonel Baden-Powell detailed an officer, Mr. Greenfield and six men to accompany the Cape Boys (who invariably opened the ball) up the river bed with orders not to fire unless sure of killing someone, because, though they thoroughly enjoyed themselves yesterday they got through an enormous quantity of powder and shot. These Cape Boys are good men, fair shots, very brave, and have accounted for quite a large number of Boers while out sniping. In consequence of these orders sniping resumed its old condition, and not many volleys were fired. Creaky, in consequence, fired rather more.

2nd. The fire of the Bechuanaland Rifles drove the Boers from their advanced trench to the north-east, which they had occupied, but subsequently abandoned and destroyed, as it was too advanced. But another trench was constructed midway between this trench and our own advanced trench. Four railway men out sniping towards Game Tree Fort, came upon the niggers the Boers had posted in advance of that earthwork, and shot one, the rest fled. The Boers swarmed into the trench and their commander was heard to order some men to go and cut the party off. Sharp came the answer, "No, the *rooineks* are attacking in force." Eventually, after crawling a thousand yards under fire, the party got off safely, having accounted for two Boers.

3rd, Sunday. As our parties were digging late Saturday night and early this morning in the vicinity of the Boer trenches the Boers sent in a flag this morning to ask if we meant to fight on Sunday. We sent back to say no. I rode round the western outpost from the outside and was much struck by the admirable way Major Godley had laid out the trenches; they were practically impregnable. I also went up to Cannon Kopje which, with infinite difficulty, has been much strengthened daily, or, I should say, nightly. We then had sports, tilting at the ring, tent-pegging, &c., two pony races, and a polo match, and all the rank and fashion of Mafeking assembled to partake of Colonel Hore's and the Protectorate Regiment's hospitality, and to "listen to the band."

The only thing that has been thoroughly levelled in Mafeking is the Polo ground, which is very fair, and the ponies surprisingly good.

Practising polo, and mounted sports, however, have been forbidden during week days, as it draws so much fire. Indeed, Creaky elevated her muzzle once during the afternoon, which caused a certain amount of sensation, as we do not exactly trust our foes, and one shell in the crowd would have secured a good bag. It was probably to show her to the Dutch ladies who drive out to their camp on Sunday. These ladies have ceased watching the effects of the shells on the town since long range volleys began. Church in the evening. Sunday is indeed a welcome fillip all round, particularly for the poor women and children, who are confined to the *laager* all the week; eleven of the latter have died since the commencement of the siege. There are services for all denominations, every Sunday; but I think the evening ones are the more plentifully attended.

4th. A quiet day; not much shelling or sniping.

5th. Shelling and sniping. A shell burst in Well's store, killing a nigger outside (at least he died afterwards), close to me. The pieces flew all about, and I had not time to analyse where they were falling; they came too quick, but it was a pretty close shave; but then there have been innumerable close shaves and marvellous little damage done to life so far. The shell passed through the roof, just below the look-out man, whom the shot threw into the air. Fortunately it exploded in the next store, otherwise no doubt he would have been blown to pieces. As I write two shells have just exploded, one blowing a *kaffir* to pieces and wrecking a chemist shop, the other knocking over a white man, who is just being removed to hospital; how much hurt I do not know. (I hear that he was killed.)

About 3 o'clock began the most tremendous rain, which lasted for two hours, the market square became a lake, the streets rivers, whilst our little Molopo developed at short notice into a raging torrent. It swept away all impedimenta, wooden bridges, & c., at once. The squadron in the river bed had to retire and Captain Fitzclarence while endeavouring to cross was nearly drowned. The seven-pounder was nearly washed away; the ammunition was. The trenches and bomb proofs were full to the brim, many of them proving to be in the beds of regular streams.

Had the Boers known or been able to seize their opportunity they might have made it very nasty for us with shell fire, but as it was they were in a worse plight than we were, as they had no dry cover for drying their clothes, and could not replace them, and when they emerged from their trenches our Maxims opened on them. The headquarters' staff set to work and had everybody fairly comfortable by 7 o'clock. Natives were at work bailing all night; dry clothes were given to those who had no change, brandy and quinine served out to all the trenches, the men sleeping in adjacent cover.

Wagons fetched up the women from the *laager*, and blankets were distributed to all who required them. As usual all rose to the occasion, and having proved themselves under fire now repeated the process under this onslaught from water. Perhaps the people who were worst off were the B.S.A.P. at Cannon Kopje. A wet night—their shelters flooded—and literally everything they possessed carried away, except their blankets, arms and the clothes they stood up in, and no shelter at all. However, take it all round, the enemy were much worse off than we, which is always consoling, and consequently being miserable, and having nothing to do, they opened a lively fire on the town generally, lasting about half an hour.

6th. Shelling and sniping as usual. It is their custom now to begin in the evening about 4, keep it up till dark, and then fire Creaky once from about 8.30 to 9 o'clock. Mr. Gerrans, town councillor, was extracting the fuse of an exploded shell—result—he was blown down and severely injured. His foreman, Green, had his foot blown off, and a passerby, Smith, a Johannesburg refugee, returning to his trench, was so injured that he died in an hour. Everybody was much depressed by this; it seemed so sad that more damage should be caused among the whites by an accident than had hitherto been the result of six weeks' shelling by the enemy's heavy gun. However, since artillery has been invented mankind will tamper with loaded shells, in spite of all warnings, orders, or entreaties to the contrary.

7th. Lady Sarah Wilson arrived this morning, having been exchanged for Viljoen who had been sentenced to six months' imprisonment before the war began. He, I fancy, will look fatter and in better condition than his friends outside, and did not appear over keen to join them. This plucky lady was received with loud cheers when she entered the town; she has indeed had a bad time, and everybody was greatly relieved to see her back safely, though perhaps this is not quite the best place that I know of to have a villa residence. As she drove up to her house the firing commenced again—they did not waste much time. Heavy shelling continued after dark. Three men killed, eight wounded.

Apropos of shells, I presume in the course of his life Colonel Baden-Powell has had many curious communications, but certainly none more curious than this one. The other morning a *kaffir* picked up an unexploded five-pound shell; when the fuse was unscrewed, instead of a charge the following missive was found:—

Mr. Baden-Powell,
Pleas excuse me for sending this iron messenger i have no other to send at Present. He is rather exentric but vorgive him if he does not behave well i wish to ask you not to let your men drink all the whisky as i wish to have a drink when we all come to see you. cindly tell Mrs. Dunkley that her mother and vamily are all quite well.

I remaijn,

Yours trewly, a Republican.

I am afraid the ingenious gentleman in question will have to wait a while for his whisky.

8th. Quiet all the morning; but this afternoon shell fire began, killing one man, Protectorate Regiment, and wounding two. Creaky only fired one round, our snipers keeping her quiet; but sniping all round made things pretty lively.

9th. Pretty quiet; not much shell fire in the morning, but began in the evening, and pretty smart sniping continued all day. I must now endeavour to describe the hospital arrangements, and the noble work done by the ladies of Mafeking. The hospital arrangements for the defence of the town were made under the supervision of Dr. Haves, Major Anderson, R.A.M.C., and Surgeon Holmden assisting him; Major Anderson being attached to the Protectorate Regiment, which might have been moved at any time. In addition to being under a hot fire the whole of the first fight, he accompanied the ambulance to Cannon Kopje, during the fight there. Bullets whistled round the Red Cross the whole way there and round the stretchers (which he assisted to carry) on their return to the shelter of the railway embankment.

There may have been some excuse for firing on the Red Cross during the first fight, on the second occasion there can have been none; probably the Boers considered that we adopted the same practice as themselves and brought up our ammunition in ambulances. Whether this is a valid excuse or not, I will leave my readers to decide. The Red Cross flag, at the commencement of the siege floated over the railway embankment, the first dressing station, the refugee camp dressing station, the women's *laager*, Messrs. Weil's (who had placed their house at the disposal of the authorities for the use of the wounded), the convent, which is fitted up as a hospital, and the Victoria Hospital.

General Cronje stated, and with some show of reason, that he could only recognize one hospital, and the women's *laager*. However, prior to this, he had sent many shells through the convent, possibly from its being a two-storied building and naturally a conspicuous mark. Consequently Victoria Hospital, always the main hospital, became the only one used throughout the operations. Dr. Haves was the P.M.O., Miss Hill the matron; and here, on behalf of the garrison of Mafeking, I must endeavour to convey our feelings of deep gratitude and admiration for the work done by this lady, the nurses, and their assistants (the ladies of Mafeking) during the siege. I can testify personally to their devoted care and attention to patients, and Britain may well be proud of them.

One ninety-four pounder went through the hospital, wrecking a ward and killing a little native boy. Shells fell all round it, and bullets were continually hitting it, one, indeed, wounded an already wounded man, but these ladies continued their work undisturbed, assisted to the utmost by the sisters from the adjacent convent, situated some fifty yards away. These poor ladies having had to abandon their home (which was literally wrecked, and will have to be entirely rebuilt), had to take refuge in a dug-out by the hospital. The hospital arrangements and the attention of Dr. Haves, Major Anderson, and Surgeon Holmden (who was himself sick in the hospital), were beyond all praise. Fortunately the accommodation was adequate, an additional building being erected for *kaffirs*. But these for the most part preferred being treated and returning to their own abode. They appear nearly insensible to pain.

To give a few instances, one native was shot with a Martini bullet through the lung; he roared with laughter when it was extracted, and will not part with it for anything, and is now all right. A Zulu wounded in the toe, on seeing a man's temperature being taken, when given the thermometer, placed it between his toes, and on being told to put it in his mouth, said he was not hurt in the mouth, but in the foot. Another native was shot through the head with a Mauser and lived; so, indeed, did a railway volunteer, Nelson; the bullet went clean through his head, and he is well and out of hospital. But the natives, though suffering from horrible injuries, seem to regard them lightly.

Most of the native wounded are by shells; they are very careless, but I fancy the numerous casualties are making them more cautious. The unfortunate man killed yesterday was a man named Footman, of the Protectorate Regiment, who was in a room singing a song, "Poor old Joe has gone to rest," to the accompaniment of a banjo, when the shell burst on him, and literally blew him to pieces—two more men were slightly injured, and a chaff-cutter knocked to pieces; but the remainder were providentially untouched. The worst of sniping is that it consumes such a lot of the ammunition which we may eventually require, though it certainly has a quietening effect upon the enemy's artillery; but I cannot believe the Boers will abandon this place without one more serious attack, when they hear of the advance of our troops, and the remnants of other commandoes join them.

They must have one tangible proof of success. So far, beyond doubt, the prolonged defence of Mafeking has resulted in the natives either keeping quiet or rising on our side, whereas had the Boers been successful in these parts, the natives must have perforce sided with them, as their emissaries had strained every nerve to induce them to do, prior to the war. I sincerely trust that the penalties of treason will be rigidly enforced, and that if not death, at least outlawry and confiscation will be inflicted on the Colonial Dutch who have risen, for no man has a right to a vote who has deliberately risen in British territory and fought against Her Majesty.

The Transvaal is another matter, though they have raided our territory, burnt farms, and looted cattle and annexed British Bechuanaland—that is a matter for settlement by the government and not for individuals to suffer. If the Boers are well thrashed, and they have fought well, the two nationalities will soon settle down together. But a Dutchman, or at least the lower classes (which correspond, after all, to poor whites of America with this difference, that they have a lot of black blood in them), cannot understand anything but a good licking. Disarm them rigorously, and give them a just government and they will soon peacefully acquiesce therein. But pack the Hollander-cum-German official back to his own country. South Africa is no place for them. Let them try the South American Republics; with their venal habits, they will be thoroughly at home.

A more heterogeneous garrison has seldom been collected. A mounted corps (the Protectorate Regiment), two detachments of mounted Cape Police, the B.S.A.P., also mounted, the Bechuanaland Rifles, the Railway D.W., and the Town Guard, all employed in trenches, and the horses only used for orderly work. The Town Guard is composed of every white man or householder, Indian or otherwise, capable of bearing arms, unless enrolled under the Red Cross. They are formed into companies in their own districts, and under their own commanders, Colonel Vyvyan being commander of the whole, and range from boys of sixteen to men of seventy. The younger boys are employed as messengers. The Town Guard have been subjected to severe tests, sleeping and living in trenches, and enduring the hardships of war for two months, without a chance of returning the enemy's fire.

A few individuals who are good shots are permitted to go out sniping, but the majority have to keep their fire for short ranges, in case of an assault. They have done their duty well, and been under fire continually. All sorts and conditions of men are there, and a more mixed body it would be impossible to conceive. In any case, they have stood the test well, and surprised myself and indeed everybody by their efficiency. Of the police of both corps, it is impossible to say too much—they are as fine a body of men as you could wish to see, and the work they have done speaks for itself. The B.S.A.P. have had the more opportunities as a body, but wherever the Cape Police have had a chance they have done every bit as well. The Protectorate Regiment I have already described fully, and they also have proved themselves to be the fine fighting material I thought them from the first. But when, oh! when, shall we use our horses? The Bechuanaland Rifles, a fine body of men, largely augmented since the commencement of the war, had a mounted detachment under Captain Cowell.

The Railway Division under Captain Moore, who has been promoted since the commencement of the war, are also a fine body of men who can turn their hand to anything, from fighting in a land ironclad to manning their own works. The authorities were warned long prior to the outbreak of hostilities, that more troops were required here. With even two squadrons of cavalry and half a battery we should have been able to keep the Boers at a greater distance from the town, and beaten them occasionally in the open, well away from our lines. Half a battalion of infantry would have done the garrison work as efficiently as the dismounted men of our mounted corps. In fact, we might long ago have raised the siege by a decisive blow, which we have been, under our present circumstances, unable to deliver. I think I stated this in a letter some six weeks prior to the outbreak of the war. However, I presume we shall soon be out of this now, though we have no news, as for the past fortnight no runners seem able to get through at all.

10th, Sunday. We had mounted sports, polo, and in the evening, church. Heavy rain threatened, but held off. I watched through a telescope a party of Dutch ladies being shown Creaky, who was put through her antics, being elevated, depressed, levelled in various directions, for their benefit. So, both sides enjoyed themselves after their kind.

General Snyman's harangues and reports of victories (which roughly surmised are—extirpation of the British army—the only two places in South Africa held by the British, being Mafeking and Cape Town—possession of Delagoa Bay, and a fight at sea, where the British were defeated) are now received in silence and *cum grano*, by his followers, instead of being greeted with cheers, as formerly. Really, I begin to believe there is a limit to the credulity of the Boer, though hitherto I had supposed it boundless. But what can equal their colossal impudence, in invading the *suzerain* power, annexing Bechuanaland, and proclaiming us rebels. Colonel Baden-Powell has recently organized a troop of old cavalry soldiers, and armed them with lances. They have today ridden all round the town, showing themselves in all quarters, to the great astonishment of the Boers, who, I suppose, now expect another little surprise packet, and will be anxious for a few days; as they knew we had no lances with us.

11th, Monday. Colonel Baden-Powell has issued a proclamation calling upon all *burghers* to return to their farms by the 14th, and that if they do so, and surrendered their rifles and one hundred and fifty rounds of ammunition, they will not be molested, otherwise, they will be treated most rigorously, when we take the offensive; that they are being grossly misled by their leaders; that foreign intervention is hopeless. The Staats Artillery may surrender as prisoners of war at any time; this does not apply to British subjects, traitors or deserters. This might have produced an increase of shell fire, I should fancy, judging from our heavy days' shelling last week. Their general rode forth with his escort, our snipers placed three volleys round him, whereupon he galloped back to the big gun, and all the artillery began merrily, trying to hit our headquarters. They fired a few shells this morning, but the heavy rain seriously damped their ardour.

Still, if the general be annoyed, they will probably recommence their attentions. Later. The orderlies with the various flags of truce, have returned, proclamations were sent to each of their outworks, and all the Dutchmen volunteered that they were quite sick of it, and had had enough, which I can quite believe. The rains are beginning, they complained of the soakings they have already had, and with inadequate cover sickness will soon play havoc with them. The orderlies gave them cigarettes and conversed with them, and in two or three cases they asked them how they came to let the reinforcements in, referring to the lancer troop. In one case the Dutchman said he had heard them come in, but did not know what it was, in the other cases they said they had not seen the reinforcements, but they had seen their spoor. Shelling has recommenced. Tonight we send up fire balloons, weather permitting, which will probably produce some effect on their side.

The following is a copy of Colonel Baden-Powell's letter to Snyman and the proclamation to the *burghers*:—

A LETTER TO THE BOERS.

Mafeking, 8th Dec., 1899.

To General J. P. Snyman,
near Mafeking.

Sir,—I beg to thank you for having handed over Lady Sarah Wilson in exchange for the convict P. Viljoen.

At the same time, I beg to point out that I have only consented to the exchange under protest, as being contrary to the custom of civilised warfare.

In treating this lady as a prisoner of war, as well as in various other acts, you have in the present campaign, altered the usual conditions of war. This is a very serious matter; and I do not know whether it has the sanction of General Joubert or not, but I warn you of the consequences.

The war was at first, and would remain, as far as Her Majesty's troops are concerned, a war between one government and another; but you are making it one of people against people in which women are considered as belligerents. I warn you that the consequence of this may shortly be very serious to your own people, and you yourself will be to blame for anything that may happen.

Regarding your complaint as to your being attacked by natives, I beg to refer you to my letter dated 14th November, addressed to your predecessor General Cronje. In this letter I went out of my way, as one white man to another, to warn you that the natives are becoming extremely incensed at your stealing their cattle, and the wanton burning of their *kraals*; they argued that the war lay only between our two nations, and that the quarrel had nothing to do with themselves, and they had remained neutral in consequence, excepting in the case of the Mafeking Baralongs, who had to defend their homes in consequence of your unjustifiable invasion.

Nevertheless you thought fit to carry on cattle thefts and raids against them, and you are now beginning to feel the consequences; and, as I told you, I could not be responsible. And I fear from what I have just heard by wireless telegraph that the natives are contemplating further operations should your forces continue to remain within or on the borders of their territories.

Before the commencement of the war the High Commissioner issued stringent orders to all natives that they were to remain quiet and not to take up arms unless their territory were invaded (in which case, of course, they had a perfect right to defend themselves).

Linchwe—of whom you complain—remained neutral until you brought a force into his principal town and looted his traders' stores, and were making preparations for shelling his *stadt* on the 26th *ultimo*. Having obtained accurate information of these intentions of yours, and warned by what had happened to the natives near Mafeking, he attacked your *laager* on the 24th in order to save his town from being shelled and consequent loss of life amongst his women and children. In this I consider he was quite justified, and you have no one but yourself to blame in the matter.

While on the subject of natives please do not suppose that I am ignorant of what you have been doing with regard to seeking the assistance of armed natives, nor of the use of the natives by you in the destruction of the railway line south of Mafeking. However, having done my duty in briefly giving you warning on these points, I do not propose to further discuss them by letter.

    I have the honour to be,

        Sir,

            Your obedient servant,

                R.S.S. Baden-Powell.

NOTICE

To the *Burghers* of the Z.A.R. at Present Under Arms Near Mafeking.

From the Officer Commanding Her Majesty's Forces, Mafeking.

Burghers,—I address you in this manner because I have only recently learnt how you are being intentionally kept in the dark by your officers and your government newspapers as to what is really happening in other parts of South Africa.

As officer commanding Her Majesty's troops on this border I think it right to point out to you clearly the inevitable result of your remaining any longer in arms against Great Britain.

You are all aware that the present war was caused by the invasion of British territory by your forces, and as most of you know, without any justifiable reason.

Your leaders do not tell you that so far your forces have met with what is only the advanced guard of the British force, and that circumstances have changed within the past week; the main body of the British is now daily arriving by thousands from England, Canada, India, and Australia, and is about to advance through your country. In a few weeks the South African Republic will be in the hands of the English; no sacrifice of life on your part can stop it. The question now to put to yourselves before it is, is this: Is it worth while losing your lives in a vain attempt to stop their invasion or to take a town beyond your borders which, if taken, would be of no use to you? (And I may tell you that Mafeking cannot be taken by sitting down and looking at it, for we have ample supplies for several months to come).

The Staat Artillery have done us very little damage, and we are now well protected with forts and mines. Your presence here, or elsewhere, under arms, cannot stop the British advancing into your country.

Your leaders and newspapers are also trying to make you believe that some foreign continental powers are likely to intervene in your behalf against England. This is not in keeping with their pretence that your side is going to be victorious, nor is it in accordance with facts. The S.A.R. having declared war and taken the offensive cannot claim intervention on its behalf. And were it not so, the German emperor is at present in England, and fully in sympathy with us: the American Government have

41

warned others of their intention to side with England should any other nation interfere; France has large interests in the gold fields identical with those of England; and Italy is entirely in accord with us; and Russia sees no cause to interfere.

The war is a war of one government against another and not of people against people. The duty assigned to my troops is to sit still here until the proper time arrives and then to fight and to kill until you give in. You, on the other hand, have other interests to think of, in your families and farms and their safety.

Your leaders have caused the destruction of farms in this country and have fired on women and children, and our men are becoming hard to restrain in consequence. Your leaders have also caused invasion of *kaffir* territory, and looting of their cattle, and have thus induced them to rise, and in their turn to invade your country, and to kill your *burghers*.

As one white man to another, I warned General Cronje on the 14th November that this would occur, and yesterday I heard that more *kaffirs* are rising, and are contemplating similar moves; and I have warned Snyman accordingly. Thus great bloodshed, and destruction of farms threaten you on all sides, and I wish to offer you a chance of avoiding it. To this end my advice to you is to return without delay to your homes and there remain peacefully till the war is over. Those of you who do this before the 14th instant will be as far as possible protected, as regards yourselves, your families, and property, from confiscations, looting, and other penalties to which those who remain under arms may be subjected when the invasion takes place.

Our secret agents will communicate to me the names of those who do and of those who do not avail themselves, before the 13th instant, of the terms now offered. To ensure their property being respected, all the men of a family must be present at home when the troops arrive and be prepared to hand over a rifle and 150 rounds of ammunition each.

The above terms do not apply to officers or to members of the Staats Artillery, who may surrender as prisoners of war at any time; nor do they apply to rebels from British territory or others against whom there may be other charges. It is probable that my force will shortly again take the offensive.

To those who, after this warning, defer their submission till too late, I can offer no promise, and they will only have themselves to blame for an injury or loss of property that they or their families may afterwards suffer.

(Signed)   R.S.S. Baden-Powell,
                                  Colonel.

Mafeking, 10th Dec., 1899.

The proclamation has either had a good effect or it is a curious coincidence, that, since its issue, the town has been barely shelled at all, sniping has almost ceased, and the Boers have only shelled the trenches in front of the native location, and the location itself, in a perfunctory manner, the result being that though we have shot a few Boers, our casualties have been nil, except some natives in the location, and from the 12th to the 15th nothing worth mentioning has happened. I fancy their news from the south must be bad, and undoubtedly men and cattle have gone away lately. Thanks to their recent vigilance, our native runners have failed to get through, and I imagine the same fate has befallen the runners trying to come in, for we have been absolutely without reliable news for the last three weeks. General Snyman sent in a copy of the *Volkstem*, relating our enormities and their victories, all underlined. I am bound to say the news was taken with much salt; but still it was news of a sort. The leading articles were mainly whining for foreign intervention, so we could read between the lines.

15th. Later. I was somewhat previous in my remarks, they have just placed a shell within a hundred yards of the hotel.

December 16th. (Dingaan Day.) We were aroused at 2.39 a.m. by the Boers celebrating their independence. They sent a ninety-four pounder through the corner of Dixon's Hotel, which is our headquarters, consequently all rooms and passages are full of sleepers, the orderlies sleeping in the passages and billiard room. However, fortunately they managed to put their shell through the bar, which is the only empty room in the house, and wrecked a portion of it and the *stoep*, which by day is full of occupants. A splinter stopped the town clock, hence the accuracy with which we timed our unlooked-for alarum. They have tried to hit headquarters for some weeks, shells pitching all round the hotel and wrecking neighbouring buildings, but heretofore we had escaped. Then, having drawn their bow at a venture by night, they have at last succeeded in hitting it.

After having inspected the damage I turned in again. But as our seven-pounder at Cannon Kopje returned the fire, it became universal, and I think the Boers intended to attack. Colonel Baden-Powell having anticipated something of the sort, had had the little gun laid on their big one the night before. As it was impossible to sleep, I went down to Ellis's corner to join in the fun. For nearly three weeks we had let them fire away without taking much notice of them. Today, however, knowing it was their national festival, we were determined to disturb their amusement.

Our old seven-pounders had their advanced trenches well in range, and three of them, about three-quarters of a mile apart, commenced playing havoc with the said trenches, shells bursting beautifully in and over them. While Creaky, like a big dog annoyed by little ones, snapped hurriedly at each of its puny antagonists in turn. It made better practice than I have yet seen, and burst its huge shells within fifteen and twenty yards of the guns. When the smoke from its muzzle was seen, our gun detachments laid down, but the explosion and smoke of the big shells had not died away before "boom," through the smoke, came the derisive return of its tiny antagonist, showing "a miss to the Boers." The guns took no notice of Creaky after the first shot, but concentrated their attention on the trenches, leaving her to be soothed by musketry volleys. Our shell fire had a most quieting effect on the occupants of the trenches, and we had to stir them up by sniping their individuals, and then when they woke up a bit the Maxims assisted in calming their unruly spirits again.

Altogether a most enjoyable morning. It is so dull being shot at without answering, but when one's own guns keep the game going, it is quite another thing. This lasted till about 6.30. Just to prevent their being too much taken up by any amusements they might have contemplated, to celebrate the day, our guns fired a few rounds again at noon, but the big gun only answered with a few rounds, and after a feeble spatter of musketry we knocked off. On the western front, about dusk, our seven-pounder, under Captain Sandford, knocked out their five-pounder, and they dismantled their fort and withdrew to a more retired position.

We have advanced our seven-pounder to Fort Ayr, and hope to repeat the process. The first of our shells burst right among them whilst they were outside making coffee.

17th, Sunday. We had a handicap polo tournament. Here are the teams and the result from *The Mafeking Mail:*—

No. 1.—Colonel Baden-Powell (Captain),
Captain Gordon Wilson,

REMOVING THE EFFECTS OF A BOER SHELL.

Captain Singleton,
Lieutenant Hon. A. Hanbury-Tracey.

No. 2.—Captain Lord C. Cavendish-Bentinck (Captain),
Lieutenant-Colonel Walford,
Major Anderson,
Lieutenant Mackenzie.

No. 3.—Lieutenant-Colonel Hore (Captain),
Captain Sandford,
Captain Vernon,
Lieutenant Bridges.

No. 4.—Major Godley (Captain),
Major Goold-Adams, C.B., C.M.G.,
Captain Fitzclarence,
Lieutenant Moncreiffe.

No. 5.—Major Baillie (Captain),
Captain Marsh,
Captain Cowan,
Lieutenant Paton.

Match.		Goals scored.
1	Colonel Hore	1
	Lord C. Bentinck	1
2	Colonel Baden-Powell	0
	Major Godley	1
3	Lord C. Bentinck	1
	Major Baillie	1
4	Colonel Baden-Powell	0
	Colonel Hore	1
5	Major Godley	0
	Major Baillie	2
6	Lord C. Bentinck	0
	Colonel Baden-Powell	1
7	Major Godley	1
	Colonel Hore	1
8	Major Baillie	0
	Colonel Baden-Powell	1
9	Lord C. Bentinck	1
	Major Godley	0
10	Major Baillie	1
	Colonel Hore	0

	Total goals scored.
Colonel Baden-Powell's team	2
Captain Lord C. Bentinck's team	3
Lieutenant-Colonel Hore's team	3
Major Baillie's team	4
Major Godley's team	2

Colonel Baden-Powell's team had a captain who played an excellent game. Major Baillie was decidedly the mainstay of his team, not only by the unerring accuracy with which he hit the ball, but also on account of the verbal assistance delivered unceasingly in stentorian tones to his side.

We are now making great preparations for Christmas, which we are apparently condemned to spend here. Church services as usual.

18th. A quiet day; except on the western front, where their five-pounder keeps pegging away; however, no one takes any notice of it, as our new gun-pit is not yet completed. Tomorrow we hope to have another lively morning. The Boers have been drilling, apparently practising an attack formation, somewhat late in the day, however, and not of much use now, as they could not get in if they tried, and they are not likely to make the attempt. As I before said, Colonel Baden-Powell has collected some thirty lances and armed a troop with them, so that, if the enemy depart hurriedly, we may be able to speed them on their way. Went sniping in the evening; they fired the one-pound Maxim and a good deal of musketry fire. Our troops in the advance trenches had quite good shooting all day.

19th. As I anticipated. The Boers' *reveille* was sounded for them at 4.30 a.m. by our seven-pounders, which made excellent practice on the brickfield trench. Their big gun repeated its performance of Saturday harmlessly. We shifted them from their trenches and turned Maxims on them, while the Nordenfeldt at long range volleys pestered their big gun. Their one-pound Maxim fire was wild, but they slew an inoffensive jackass. This lasted until about 6, and was very pretty. At about 7 Creaky began to fire at Cannon Kopje, but without effect; she shot straighter in the morning; and at about 9 our seven-pounders began again, but the enemy would not be drawn, and now only occasional dropping shots come idly from both sides.

On the western front our seven-pounder silenced the five-pounder at Game Tree Fort. On the eastern front the race-course trench much annoyed the gun under Major Panzera, with volleys, till kept under by the convent Maxim and our one-pound Maxim. These two artillery fights cannot much impress the Boers with the extraordinary value of the much belauded ten-tonner, and must destroy her moral effect, for whichever of our guns she fires at immediately returns her fire. However, she has annoyed us quite enough and done sufficient damage to life and property, but if we had only had a gun which could have reached her properly, we should have knocked her out long ago.

A duel between our Nordenfeldt and Creaky began this afternoon, and has since been of daily occurrence, amidst the laughter and applause of the spectators. No sooner has the big shell struck, than crack, crack, comes from the Nordenfeldt. Indeed, of late the little gun fires when the smoke from Creaky's muzzle appears, and gets off its three shots before the arrival of the shell, which the gunners of the monster do not seem to appreciate at all. It is a regular case of dignity and impudence with the laugh on the side of impudence. In the evening Captain Sandford silenced the Boer gun on the western front.

20th and 21st. Quiet days.

22nd. Quiet, but furious musketry fire at night, bullets flying everywhere.

23rd. Saturday. Fairly quiet.

I broke my head taking a fall at polo, which we now play two or three times a week; it is a new experience going to and from the polo ground under fire.

24th, Sunday. Owing to siege exigencies it was deemed necessary to hold our Christmas on the Sunday, as the Boers' religious festival is held on New Year's Day. All creeds held their ordinary church services. Lady Sarah Wilson and Mr. B. Weil had organized a Christmas tree and tea for the two hundred and fifty children of Dutch and English parentage who were in the town. Brakes were running to and from the *laager*, filled with children, shrilly cheering and waving the Union Jack, the most effective one run by poor Captain Vernon, who was killed within forty-eight hours. The children seemed thoroughly to enjoy themselves, and great thanks are due to the organizers of the *fête* and their assistants, for everyone was pleased to see the children enjoy themselves. For the adults, sports were held, and a cheerful Christmas Day was passed.

Christmas Day. All creeds held their usual Christmas services though under some difficulty, as everyone was on duty, though the Boers kept Christmas as Sunday; yet it was no certainty to commence with. The Rev. Mr. Weekes, the Church of England clergyman, had to play the harmonium, as well as conduct the service.

26th. The myriads of locusts which had lately devastated our grazing grounds, already insufficient for the large number of cattle in and about the town, had rendered it imperative that some steps should be taken to raise our close investment sufficiently to obtain an extended field for grazing secure from attack or raid. This was sufficient reason for action in itself, but in addition, the approach of our forces to Gaberones in the north, made it advisable to prepare to open up the line and endeavour to join hands with them, and thus by extending our perimeter and line of forts to throw additional work on the investing force, and so prevent reinforcements being sent to the commandoes acting against our troops north and south; nay, we even hoped to draw reinforcement from these commandoes to assist in maintaining the strict investment which the Boers deemed it so necessary to retain around Mafeking.

Accordingly, Colonel Baden-Powell decided to attack Game Tree Fort, which commands the line to the north. And now, before going further with an account of the fight, let me say that in spite of great secrecy, as to the time or place of attack, the Boers, through treachery, were forewarned and forearmed as to our intentions. The garrison was doubled, and the fort from an open earthwork turned into a blockhouse with three tiers of fire, while the line was broken in the night between the fort and the town, preventing the efficient co-operation of the armoured train. On Christmas night, at about 11 o'clock, the chief of the staff, Lord Edward Cecil, collected the correspondents and told them of the intended attack, advising them to rendezvous at 3 o'clock, with the headquarters at Dummie Fort.

The plan of attack was as follows:—C squadron, Protectorate Regiment, were to take up a position during the night near the railway to the west of Game Tree Fort, supported by D squadron, under Captain Fitzclarence, and the armoured train with a Hotchkiss and Maxim, under Captain Williams, B.S.A.P. The right flank being protected by the Bechuanaland Rifles, under Captain Cowan. The whole of the right attack under Major Godley. The left attack being composed of three seven-pounder guns, one cavalry Maxim, and one troop, Lord Charles Bentinck's A squadron, Protectorate Regiment, under Major

Panzera, with the other two troops in support, the whole left attack being under Colonel Hore. The Dummie Fort lay midway between the two attacks. The wait from 3 o'clock seemed interminable, but at 4.28 the first gun fired, and then our seven-pounder shells burst merrily over the fort.

The infantry commenced volleys and the Maxim joined in. The armoured train was stopped by the broken line some half mile from where it could have efficiently co-operated, and the squadrons commenced their attack from the railway line, D being echeloned some three hundred yards in the rear of C. From the Dummie Fort the attack could be perfectly seen, as it advanced rapidly across our front. The rushes were well made, and the charge in perfect order, the leaders racing in front of their men right up to the fort, where the firing for a while ceased, and then broke out again with renewed vigour. From where I was, I thought the attacking squadron had secured the position, and, from the slowness and deliberation with which the men retired, that the supporting squadron was falling back to its lines, as, with the smokeless powder, we could not see our men firing, and the sound was drowned in the rattle of Boer musketry.

This, alas, was not the case. Captain Vernon, who had been wounded in the advance, led his men most gallantly up to the work, to find it with three tiers of loopholes and an iron roof, the bushes in front concealing this until right on to the fort. Here he and Lieutenant Paton and fifteen men fell, and his sergeant-major mortally wounded. Captain Sandford had been shot twice just short of the work, but called on his men to charge. These were the last words he spoke, and only four of the men of his troop were not placed *hors de combat*. Captain Fitzclarence had also fallen wounded, before reaching the work, but I am glad to say is doing well. With this spirit shown by the officers and responded to by the men, small wonder that we may be proud of the attack, even though unsuccessful in obtaining possession of the work, and that the Boers afterwards seemed more depressed than ourselves. They knew the men they had to deal with.

Corporal Cooke got on the roof of the work, and had four bullets through his tunic, but was untouched. Mr. Paton and Sergeant-Major Paget were shot whilst firing with their revolvers through the loopholes (the Boers still speak of Paton's courage), and so were many men. After the retirement, the stretcher parties went out, and the Boers assisted in succouring our wounded, and behaved on the whole very well, though some young roughs got out of hand and plundered the dead and wounded. Their leaders behaved exceedingly well, and did their best to restrain them.

I went up there and a more ghastly collection of wounds could not be imagined, mostly shot at the muzzles of the rifles in the head, and in some cases with large Boer bullets. Death must have been instantaneous. The field cornets told me they had been expecting the attack, and the rapidity with which reinforcements arrived—the presence of General Snyman, and several leaders, and the destruction of the line, together with the increase of the garrison, tend to endorse their statements. Our wounded were all wounded in front, some of the men retiring backwards so as not to be shot in the back. Sergeant Barry, mortally wounded, sent word to his mother that he had three wounds all in front. Our force was under one hundred actually attacking. The Boers when reinforced about four hundred.

Our losses killed or since dead: Captain Vernon, Captain Sandford, Lieutenant Paton, twenty-one rank and file; wounded: Captain Fitzclarence, twenty-two rank and file; four prisoners. The men retiring were quite cool and willing to have another go—smoking and laughing in some cases, but in the majority bitter and angry at not having got in. British troops have certainly performed as fine feats of arms, but no more determined attack with inferior numbers against an enemy armed with modern rifles in a strong position has ever been pushed home, or a more deliberate and gallant retirement under heavy fire been made.

The enemy were much impressed, and said they had never seen such brave men, and though we failed in taking the fort, the action has resulted in the enemy daily strengthening every work, and upset them greatly, as they hourly anticipate a fresh attack, and gusts of musketry break out from their lines at night, for no apparent reason. Indeed, the rapidity with which their white flags were hoisted on the arrival of our ambulances make me, in my own mind, absolutely certain that they were prepared to contemplate surrender, and in any case they will certainly not be able to spare men from this place to assist their retiring commandoes. Altogether their rash and insolent advance into British territory has placed them here, as elsewhere, in about as unpleasant a position for irregular troops as can well be imagined. In the evening we buried our dead.

The Protectorate Regiment, after a life of four months, and a strength of four hundred, has now suffered one hundred and ten casualties. It has accordingly had to be reorganised from four squadrons into three. On no occasion has it been engaged without distinguishing itself, and I think in its last action, though repulsed, it has, if possible, distinguished itself most.

What I have said about the contemplated surrender of the Boers has since been confirmed by what I heard on my journey south towards Vryburg. Keely, now Resident Magistrate in these parts, had been taken into camp about this time to swear neutrality; and the Boers made no secret of their intention to surrender the fort; but they were kept up to the mark by one determined man, who, lying behind an ammunition box, swore he would blow out the brains of the first man who offered to surrender. It was at this man that Paton was firing through a loophole with a pistol when he was shot. Nobody else on our side seems to have spotted the individual in question, hence the Boers, on our retiring, continued the fight.

27th, 28th, and 29th. Desultory shelling, sniping, and occasional wild firing from the enemy by night. We hear cheering native rumours from the south.

31st, Sunday. Sports, &c., driving competition, horse-show. I won hack competition.

January 1st, 1900, New Year's Day. We had anticipated a quiet day, as this is a Boer festival. I presume they thought we anticipated this, for they commenced early with a heavy bombardment and experimented with incendiary bombs, which however were of no success. A valuable member of the garrison, one of our few carpenters, Slater by name, was killed.

2nd. Our usual shelling, and a niece of a Baralong chief killed in the *stadt*, amongst others. In the evening Mr. Hamilton, *Times* correspondent, gave the staff and the other correspondents a most excellent dinner, which we all thoroughly appreciated, at Riesle's Hotel. How so good a dinner could be served after about four months' siege is indeed extraordinary.

3rd. The quick Q.-F. Krupp was moved to the north-west of the town, and fired on the western forts, amongst other places into the women's *laager*, killing two children, one Dutch, one English.

4th. Typhoid has broken out in the women's *laager*. I suppose we may consider ourselves lucky it is not more prevalent. The usual shelling goes on.

5th. Enemy quiet, with the usual shelling, which is terribly monotonous.

6th. Boers rather vicious today, and the usual Saturday's spar all round at sundown. Runners went north and south.

7th, Sunday. In the early morning heavy musketry fire from the Boers, quite contrary to their usual custom. Sports, Christie Minstrels, and a comical turn-out competition.

8th. Rained hard. Shelling went on as usual, and my usual sniping ground destroyed by four shells, and the occupant fatally injured. Shrapnel fired over the women's *laager.*

9th. From now onwards we may assume a very heavy shelling every day. Two whites and two natives injured while tampering with a hundred pound shell, one white since dead.

10th. Mrs. Poulton, born a Dutch woman, shot through the head and killed, also a few natives; this woman's sister at the commencement of the siege expressed the wish that the streets of Mafeking might run with English blood. This charming lady, named Hammond, created so much disturbance at the commencement of the siege that she was put under restraint; her daughter has since been severely wounded. Curses, like chickens, come home to roost.

11th. Usual day of shelling.

12th. A Boer attack on Fort Ayr. They galloped wildly fifty yards in advance of their trenches, about one thousand five hundred yards from Fort Ayr, and indulged in a fantasia, but never came any nearer. Their guns, however, five, twelve, and one hundred pounders, shot very straight and shelled for two hours. Our casualties, one man wounded, since dead.

13th. Big gun did not fire, enemy very quiet; expect they are running short of small arm ammunition.

14th, Sunday. Great excitement caused by disappearance of Creaky, many rumours. She was seen in at least six different places, but we all hoped she had taken a fond farewell.

15th. Creaky actually discovered about two miles down the Malmani Road. She had apparently been moved by our persistent persecutions, and we thought she had been moved into a worse position for her. We have materially changed our minds, at any rate, at the eastern end of the town, where she fires regularly at meal times, mostly hitting hotels. She commenced firing at 11 o'clock.

16th. Dislike the shelling more since I have fever; one shell struck auxiliary hospital.

17th. Enemy tried to foist *kaffirs* into the town, to further diminish our food supply, under a flag of truce. Colonel Baden-Powell refused to receive them. They fired heavily and inexplicably on our white flag carried by Ronny Moncrieffe while retreating. Tremendous indignation in the town, though there is some rumour that one of our *kaffirs* fired a shot somewhere (this was subsequently found to be untrue). Shell hit bomb proof occupied by Mr. Vere Stent, Reuter's representative, and myself. Large pieces ricocheted through Dixon's Hotel which was crowded; usual providential escapes.

18th. They shell the town as usual. Most unpleasant this end. They knocked off all corners of the square in two days; several casualties.

Our system of avoiding the gun is having look-out men in all parts, who ring so many strokes when the gun is loaded, so many when pointed, three strokes for the town, six when pointed off it. The enemy, however, have rather frustrated this, as they do not fire till uncertain intervals after the gun is pointed, ranging from an hour downwards. The lookout then rings another bell, but it gives a remarkably short time to take cover, and it is these odd shells and not a sustained shell fire which causes the loss of life; at any rate, there is no doubt that since the change of position of the gun a far greater proportion of damage has been done.

19th. There was an artillery duel between one of our seven-pounders—whose shells were made at our own factory here, and the fuses designed by Lieutenant Daniels, B.S.A.P., in which the shells and fuses proved a complete success—and the enemy's five-pounder which was almost immediately silenced. And now as regards the factory. The ammunition for the ship's gun, that weapon of our grandfathers, which was unearthed in the *stadt*, and which shoots with great violence, though doubtful precision, to enormous ranges, has been cast here. The seven-pounder's shells have been cast, studded, fused, and in every respect made perfect here. Some 2.5-pounder shells, left here by Dr. Jameson, have been fitted with two enlarged driving-bands and have been fired from our seven-pounders with complete success. Too much credit cannot be given to the ingenuity, ability, and energy with which

Conolly and all his mates have worked at strengthening that portion of our defences.

20th. The two sides when at trench work happened on each other at night in the vicinity of Fort Ayr, and we drove them back. A very effective day's shelling.

21st, Sunday. Agricultural and produce show, including babies. The first prize for foals since the commencement of the siege to Mr. Minchin, Bechuanaland Rifles; for babies, to Sergeant Brady, B.S.A.P.; a great success, and really extraordinarily good show. My fever nearly gone.

22nd. Rather late shelling today, and rumoured attack on *kaffir stadt* by Boer friendlies did not take place. A certain amount of firing from Fort Ayr. Rain begun again.

Colonel Baden-Powell protested the other day against the firing on our white flag, and General Snyman, who, as far as I could judge personally whilst in conversation with him after the action at Game Tree Fort, is a crabbed old gentleman, somewhat naturally rabidly anti-British, and according to the Boer standard an extreme martinet, sent in an answer apologising for his *burghers* having fired on the white flag, and stating with regard to Colonel Baden-Powell's remonstrance to his arming and raising the natives, that he had merely armed a few as cattle guards. In that case the Boers must have many cattle in close proximity to our camp, unseen and unknown to us.

He further stated that he had noticed us building fortifications on Sunday, to which Colonel Baden-Powell replied that we had merely taken out and relaid some mine lines, and that he had been vastly interested, while riding round the western outposts on Sunday, to see the assiduity with which the Boers had been working at their new fortifications in that part.

23rd. The usual sniping continues on the western front, but peace, punctuated occasionally by one-hundred pound shell, is more or less prevalent on the eastern. As regards our food supply, luxuries purchased at store are a thing of the past, as the authorities have taken charge of all tinned and other eatables in the place. We have now stood four months' siege, and it seems probable that this may be indefinitely prolonged, and it is mainly owing to the private enterprise of Mr. Benjamin Weil, the representative of Julius Weil & Co. here, that we are really ready to stand, as far as provisions and stores go, as long a time again.

In addition to having supplied all the government required, he laid in large stocks on his own account, and when the history of the siege of Mafeking comes to be written, he will be found to have played by no means the least important part. In addition to the white troops employed, and to the Baralongs, who defend their own *stadt*, we have four other black contingents: the *Fingoes* under Webster, the Cape Boys under Corporal Currie, C.P., a detachment of Baralongs under Sergeant Abrahams, and the "Black Watch" under Mackenzie, a mixed Zulu crowd. These gentry, to their huge delight, are continually engaged in endeavouring, with some success, to spend as much gunpowder and spill as much blood as in them lies.

The Cape Boys, under Corporal Currie, who took charge of them after Captain Goodyear's wound, from which I am glad to say he is recovering, have done notably good service, their motto and apparently only principle being "*Don't know retiring.*" In this there is a good deal of common sense; for the Boer, though not very dangerous when faced, becomes deadly and dangerous when he can shoot quietly at you as you retire. There is another portion of our defences—or perhaps that is a misnomer, I should rather say of our forces—to which I have hitherto not alluded, and that is the excellent transport service.

All the mules were individually selected by Colonel Baden-Powell and Colonel Walford, assisted by Mr. Dunlop Smith, A.V.D., and Mr. Mackenzie, transport officer, and anybody who saw the beautiful spans of mules turned out for the driving competitions would have felt that in all cases their choice was well justified, and the condition of the mules reflected the greatest credit on the squadron leaders (for each squadron leader is responsible for his own transport), conductors and drivers, and to the care and supervision given by the two officers before mentioned. The driving was excellent, and the mules looked in the pink of condition. Rather heavy shelling, and more sniping than usual. There were several casualties, mostly natives, one shell exploding in a hut and killing and wounding most of its occupants. From this date the authorities have taken over all stores of food and drink, and nothing, even luxuries, can be obtained without an order from headquarters.

24th. Desultory shelling.

25th. There was a good deal of firing today round the western trenches. In the evening a native convicted as a spy was executed. He had been sent in to obtain full information as to the stores, forts, their garrisons, and the general disposition of the forces of the town. He quite acknowledged the justice of his sentence, but only seemed to think that it was hard lines that he should be executed before he had had time to procure any information at all. This is the third native spy executed, and the various native contingents are detailed in turn for the duty.

26th. Bradley's Hotel was partially wrecked by a shell. This is the most effective explosion we have so far had. A large piece from the shell went humming overhead beyond the B.S.A.P. fort, quite three-quarters of a mile from its bursting. There is generally time for a morning ride before the big gun commences shelling, but during the last three or four hundred yards into the town, if the bells have begun to ring, there is a certain amount of excitement in returning to the hotel, as it is to this portion of the town that the enemy generally confines his attentions about breakfast time.

Later in the afternoon, Lady Sarah Wilson and Captain Wilson, who are both now convalescent, were seated with Major Goold Adams in a passage in the upper storey of the convent, when a shell burst about four feet over their heads, covering them with a pile of bricks and rubbish, but fortunately they escaped with a few bruises. There were rumours of a contemplated attack early next morning, and the northern and western fronts accordingly stood to arms. More significance was given to the rumours in that the Dutch women in the women's *laager* unanimously sought the shelter of the bomb proofs at an early hour. It was not till the next day that the reason was patent.

27th. During my return from my morning ride the big gun fired, and I saw the shell burst somewhat short of the women's *laager*. I naturally supposed this was an accident. It was not, however, the case. The big gun commenced a rapid fire in the same direction, and the effects of the shells as they fell were heliographed back from the western heights. The messages were intercepted by our signallers, under Sergeant Moffat. They placed eight large shells in and close round the *laager*, and we now understood the reason for the Dutch women taking the cover they did. It was a most deliberate piece of barbarism; mercifully, there were no casualties.

28th, Sunday. A quiet day. I rode round the western outposts in the morning and found them considerably augmented in strength. They are now a series of bomb-proof block-houses, a zigzag approach runs from the refugee *laager* up to Fort Ayr. So approach is possible without danger (which was not so before). A thousand yards to the front of Fort Ayr the new Boer fort is plainly visible, and flies a flag we have not seen before, blue, white, and orange, with a vertical green stripe. It is possible that there may be some political significance attached to this, possibly that our friends, the Transvaalers, by uniting the two Republics, hope to get the Free State Boers to fight their battles further away from their own territory; but, after all, it is pure surmise, for we get but little news of any sort—and of political news none at all.

Due south, and about eight hundred yards away from Fort Ayr, a new fort has been constructed, commanding the bed of the Molopo, and garrisoned by Cape Police. It is about on the position of the old look-out post. In the afternoon I rode round the eastern works. A trench now runs from Ellis's corner across the river, past the gun emplacement, past Webster's Kraal, up to and beyond the Nordenfelt position. It is hard to believe with the much stronger position we now have, and the reduced number of Boers, that they will attack again; but, on the other hand, it is harder to believe that they will leave Mafeking without a desperate effort to capture it. In any case, the garrison are confident.

On the termination of evening service we sing the National Anthem. I have heard it sung in many places, the most impressive of all at St. Paul's on Jubilee day; certainly next to that occasion, I think the singing of it in Mafeking appealed to me most. For the men who were singing it on Sunday night would be fighting for it on Monday morning. And now, whilst on the subject, and having just read Mr. Kipling's poem, I hope the widows and children of the irregular troops serving out here will not be forgotten when it comes to *"pay, pay, pay."*

29th. Good news of victories from the south. It seems as if the tide had turned, and as if Old England, slow as usual, was going to forge ahead at last. Her Majesty's message was received with the deepest satisfaction here. It was a month late, but none the less acceptable for being delayed. Colonel Baden-Powell issued an order, in which he referred to the execution of the spy, and warning all persons, women included, who might be found treasonably corresponding with the enemy, that, on conviction, they would be inevitably shot; also that he regretted having to take such strong measures, but that as the enemy chose to fire on the women's laager, he should confine the Dutch prisoners in a gaol constructed in the *laager*, so that, if the enemy persisted

THE OLD NAVAL GUN AT WORK.

in their brutality, they would kill their own friends. (It was a curious coincidence that on Sunday, after Saturday's performance, there was a feeling of insecurity in the town, and most people were of opinion that in all probability the Boers would violate the Sunday truce; but when the Dutch women were seen walking about, the feeling of confidence was quickly restored.)

In the afternoon the gun bequeathed to us by Lord Nelson commenced firing on the Boer *laager* at Weasel's Springs, near the head of the waterworks—a range of something over three thousand yards. Her round shot bounded about the *veldt* through, over, short of, the *laager*, rapidly dispersing a mounted body of Boers in its proximity; for, unlike a shell, when she strikes, you have by no means done with her. The drill is somewhat complicated, but thanks to an edition of Captain Marryatt's works, we have succeeded in resuscitating this long extinct form of exercise.

30th. The results of our ancient piece's firing last night has been that the laager has shifted away, in the direction of Signal Hill, and that the Boers generally have been so busy that they have not yet found time (mid-day) to discharge their Creuzot gun. There was an alarm, last night, and the eastern front and reserve squadron were held in readiness all night. Yesterday the Boers re-established themselves on the nearest brick-kiln, and a sniping entertainment was organized for them by Corporal Currie, C.P., who has charge of the Cape Boy Post, within three hundred yards.

One Boer, who for some extraordinary reason, wore a white shirt (which he will never do again) occasionally showed his back over the edge of a shelter he was constructing for himself, acting apparently on the principle of the ostrich, Trooper Piper of the Cape Police eventually got him, and at the same moment, his friend who was firing from a loop-hole, fired at Piper; fortunately Currie, who was covering the loop-hole, fired almost simultaneously and got him too, to the huge delight of the Cape Boys; stretchers came up under the Red Cross and removed the bodies, the second man was a bearded man and a well known sniper, he was an excellent shot, and the news of his demise was received with universal pleasure by the garrison, while for the rest of the day his friends made the post very warm for its occupants.

31st. There is one effect of this continual shell fire which is perhaps undesirable, and that is the remarkable degree of selfishness it engenders. There is really nothing to do and no excitement. News is rare, and not always of the best, and with lack of the proper amount of exercise and the frequent ringing of bells, which are almost as bad as the shells themselves, tempers get short, and the solicitude on "No. 1's" account increases. However, entertainments like the one organized this evening, go far to relieve our spleen and vary the interminable monotony of the siege. We were warned in the afternoon that our artillery was going to bombard the Boer lines, and from various points of vantage numerous spectators strolled out to look on. Personally, I made my way to the trench running from Ellis's corner to the river, and selected a spot where I was well away from other people, and which commanded a good view of the Boer trench, and, above all, of the big gun, which showed clearly against the white marquees in rear of it.

At the time there was no firing going on, and cattle on both sides were being brought home. Absolute stillness reigned, only broken by the lowing of the beasts, the sounds of the poultry yards, and the barking of dogs. These, with the drowsy hum of the insects, made one feel extremely sleepy, and one might well have imagined oneself lolling between two peaceful villages at home. However, at 5.30 p.m. a change came very distinctly "o'er the spirit of the dream." Our guns commenced, three seven-pounders and the Nordenfeldt, and steadily shelled for about an hour, answered by the nine-pounder quick-firer, five-pounder Krupps, and old Creaky, who swung her nose backwards and forwards from one extremity of the eastern defences to the other, making, on the whole, moderate but extremely varied practice. As I had a pair of very strong glasses, a small cluster soon collected around me, thereby inviting the undesirable attentions of their riflemen, who, however, were pretty well engaged themselves, and consequently did not annoy us very much.

It was about as safe a performance for the onlookers as could well be imagined. The guns drew most of the fire, and were scattered over a large extent of front. One could plainly see the big gun, and when she fired our way, had ample time to get into the trench. There were no casualties on our side, but after dark the Boers, who had been much upset by this disturbance of their reliefs and feeding arrangements, commenced to shell the town, killing one man outside the newspaper offices, and contriving, in some extraordinary manner, to drop a fragment of shell down the chimney of the headquarters' staff offices. This they continued till past nine, doing no further damage, except to houses.

The Boers in the course of the day put a five-pounder shell through a portion of the hospital, and at night fired a volley into the operating room, where a patient was being examined. So we conclude that they must have lost some men during the day, which made them vicious. During the past fortnight they fired upon a flag of truce, deliberately shelled the women's *laager*, and fired on the hospital.

February 1st. Today completes the sixteenth week of the siege, and we have had plenty of shell fire to celebrate it; one big shell, I regret to say, bursting on a splinter proof at Cannon Kopje, wrecking it, and killing one man and wounding two others. These splinter proofs were a line of trenches running down towards the town from the *kopje*, and it had seemed that by no chance could they possibly be struck direct by a shell. In the evening the Boer shell fire again continued till a late hour, and the last explosion that we heard puzzled us a good deal. It subsequently transpired that Major Panzera and Corporal Carrie, with three natives, had crept up to the nearest brick-kiln, from which the Boers were unfortunately absent, and had blown it up with fifty pounds of dynamite.

This will probably keep the Boers away from that locality for a while, as they are not unnaturally very cautious of approaching any place where they suspect the presence of dynamite. A Kimberley native informed us that they stop the natives going home from the Kimberley mines and ask them if there is dynamite laid down round the town, to which the natives generally reply, "Plenty!" They seem to be having a much better time in Kimberley than we are here, as the natives say we live here like mere cats, whilst they have apparently no big gun to annoy them down there.

2nd. They began shelling later here today, so one's morning's ride was uninterrupted, but they are, however, now in full swing again. Sergeant Francis, B.S.A.P., died of wounds received at Cannon Kopje. Our usual shelling.

3rd. We sent off runners north and south. In the morning the enemy devoted his attention to the town. But in the afternoon our seven-pounder and Nordenfeldt, east of Cannon Kopje, commenced firing on the enemy, who were constructing a new trench, considerably in advance of the old position of the big gun on the S.E. heights. Consequently Creaky vigorously assailed them in turn, and the Krupp gun and the one-pound Maxim galloped from McMullen's farm to her assistance. The big gun made very good shooting, but fortunately only one man was hit, and he by a sand-bag hurled up by a shell aimed at the Nordenfeldt. The Nordenfeldt gun detachment consists of two men, Privates Lowe and Mulholland, both of the Railway Volunteers, and these two men have served this gun for months daily, often under a heavy fire directed entirely at them.

At the same time our beloved relic of Lord Nelson was engaged on the western front in bombarding the new fort in front of Fort Ayr, being answered on that front and assisted by musketry and rifle fire. The week, as usual, culminated in the customary Saturday evening flare-up all round. The big gun was cleaned and oiled for Sunday, and we thought it was all over till Monday morning. This, however, was not the case. The Boers were unusually jumpy. They treated us to incendiary shells till late, and kept up a heavy musketry fire at fitful intervals during the night. They commenced constructing a new trench in the Brickfields, and can plainly be heard working at it.

4th, Sunday. The usual quiet day. At Fort Ayr, while cleaning the Maxim, it was accidentally discharged, and the Boers promptly answered, so Mr. Greenfield, in charge of the post, strolled out to explain matters, and was met half way by the Boer representatives, who talked to him for a bit, gave him the latest news (presumably untrue), exchanged little harmless chaff, and agreed to swap newspapers for whisky. The newspapers, needless to say, contained flaming accounts of universal Boer victories, which, here, one finds it somewhat hard to credit, and they agreed to furnish similar papers next Sunday. It is curious to see in the advertisement sheets advertisements from manufacturers, stating themselves to be manufacturers to Her Majesty the Queen, to read the London letter, and a column of society chit-chat in a paper published in the capital of our enemy. However, it is an odd world.

5th. Two lots of runners came in from the north this morning. Personally, I received my first communication from home since the siege began, only a wire though. Quite a number of letters came in, but were very unequally distributed. One receiving a dozen, the vast majority none, Hanbury Tracey was exceptionally fortunate, as he received a money-lender's circular and a bill, readdressed in red ink, from his orderly room at home, and that was his sole communication. They shelled us as usual, and kept it up late. A wet night, but that did not seem to deter them. Their incendiary shells were, as usual, a failure.

6th. Shelling all day, and firing at night. Two natives were killed and

Colonel Hore, commanding Protectorate Regiment, had a narrow escape whilst returning from the Court of Summary Jurisdiction.

7th. They commenced shelling early this morning, so far with little damage. There seem regular streaks of luck in this shell fire, and sometimes we strike a very bad one, but it is really marvellous how these huge shells have done comparatively little injury to life here. From what we can gather from other places, it will be about the worst knocked about town in South Africa. The remains of some buildings have been removed and the majority will require rebuilding. Yesterday, a shell went clean through the smoke box and boiler of a locomotive, and did not explode until striking the ground beyond. One also pitched on the top of an unfortunate native in an engine ash-pit and destroyed him. The price of food has naturally risen enormously and will probably rise more. The humble *kaffir*, if he possesses a hen which lays regularly, can maintain himself and another. An egg fetches sixpence, and a *kaffir's* ration of mealie meal only comes to threepence sterling, consequently the henless *kaffir* sponges upon his more wealthy brother.

This afternoon I rode up to Cannon Kopje and arrived simultaneously with a ninety-four pound shell from the contrary direction. We did not, however, hurt each other, and I dismounted and tethered my horse under the best cover available, and to ground with me like a rabbit. They fired one or two more shells at the *kopje*, doing no harm, and we then strolled up to the lookout post to have a look at our persecutor. It was a lovely evening, and as she was then pointed on the town, one could view her proceedings with the utmost equanimity, speculating mildly as to whether she would pitch her shell on one's own bomb proof or not. The shell, however, burst prematurely, just clear of the muzzle of the gun, and we continued watching the town and the rest of the defences, all of which lie like a panorama from the Cannon Kopje lookout.

Creaky was then reloaded, and with her nose cocked high in the air, was apparently aimed in the direction of the planet Venus. As a matter of fact, however, she was aimed at Fort Ayr, and after the discharge one imagined one could trace the projectile in its flight by the hurtling sound it made; but when by sound it seemed as far as Fort Miller, one could see the strike close by Fort Ayr (which is about four miles from the gun), and yet the noise of the projectile through the air continued for some seconds longer, producing a very curious effect.

She reloaded and was again pointed on the town when slowly she swung her nose round and was pointed on us, a roar of look out from the man on duty, and the crowd of languid spectators was transformed into a body of active men, heading straight for their accustomed shelters, which having attained, they peered carefully at the gun, waiting for the smoke from the muzzle, which would be the signal for their final disappearance.

We waited and waited, but she came not, so, deciding that it was the goodnight gun, I walked back, accompanied by one of the garrison of the *kopje*, and ate my dinner at the hotel with the comforting assurance that I had last seen her directed a good mile from the dining-room.

This morning Corporal Currie and his men killed and wounded a few Boers, coming at dawn to their trenches. The Boers consequently gave us a quiet day, as their obsequies and attendant ceremonies seemed to fill in all their time; but at dark they commenced a heavy fire of small arms, shell, and vituperation, upon our advanced post, about two hundred and fifty yards from their main trench. They assure the garrison of this post that they intend to make it particularly warm for them, and it is about as warm a corner as one could well select. I rode out in the afternoon to Captain Marsh's post on the western edge of the *stadt*, we have there driven the Boers out of and occupied Fort Cronje, a mile from the western edge, and seven hundred yards from the nearest Boer fort.

This Fort Cronje commands the whole of the valley on the other side of the ridge, under cover of which the Boers used to remove their reliefs and reinforcements to and from Cronje's *laager* and the western laager. Its capture has largely extended our field for grazing. We had proposed to walk out there, but on consultation we decided not to, as one is under a pretty heavy fire in the open the last part of the journey, and one would see it better and under more favourable circumstances on the Sunday, during the truce.

Riding back, I tried a short cut, at a good pace; the Boers, however, were not quite asleep, and began sniping with marvellous ill-success, as I was about to get under cover again. Today we were informed that we must be prepared to hold out for another four months, which we are quite ready to do. The garrison and inhabitants received the intelligence with the utmost equanimity felt no earthly doubt as to the result, merely expressing extreme boredom at the prospect of four months more of such monotonous existence.

9th. A runner from the south arrived, informing us of Buller's crossing the Tugela. Comparing this news with the Boer accounts of British defeats with heavy losses on the 24th, south of Tugela, one can only conclude that they must indeed be in a bad plight when they can invent such amazingly circumstantial and appalling lies. However, I hope we are nearing the end of the last act, and "God Save the Queen." They have been quiet today, and as far as we know, no funerals to occupy them so hope and trust that they are digesting some bad news; the *kaffir* who brought the messages states that the Free Staters have had enough of it, but that Cronje will not allow them to surrender, as they had everything to lose and absolutely nothing to gain; we can well believe it.

The Kimberley correspondence is of a chatty description, refers to the weather and papers (which have not arrived), but the gist of the whole is cheerful and consequently welcome, though we should prefer news. Their food supply seems good, which is consoling. But this much is certain, that if we have to hold out another four months, the means of our doing so, in the supply line, is due to the presence of Mr. B. Weil. I wonder whether it is appreciated, even yet at home, what a stupendous and monumental liar the Boer is. The Kaffir says what he thinks you will like. The Boer, however, says what he knows he likes himself. I hope someday to read a British account of the war. The Boer account would pain me if I believed it.

10th. The enemy remained quiet, at least as regards their big gun, yesterday evening, though the now nightly fusillade began about 8 o'clock. This morning they commenced shelling late, and apparently directed their projectiles at the Mill, which works every night, protected by a traverse, at the south-eastern corner of the town. They only fired two projectiles, one of which struck Mr. J. Dall, Town Councillor, and commander of one of the Town Guard posts, full, blowing him to pieces. His wife, poor woman, who was in the women's laager, where the intelligence was abruptly conveyed by a panic stricken *kaffir* woman servant, came up semi-distracted, under the escort of the Rev. W. H. Weekes. It was, of course, impossible that she should see him, and the scene was a very painful one for her friends in their endeavours to be of some comfort to her.

Musketry and the discharge of field pieces continued all the afternoon, during which we had an exceedingly heavy thunderstorm which flooded some of the uncompleted and advanced trenches, compelling the evacuation of the one within two hundred yards of the Boer main trench, during which operation one of our men was wounded. The others remained there, and sought the best cover from fire they could in its immediate propinquity. Firing continued all round the outposts, at intervals all night and well into the dawn on Sunday morning. Since we have been warned to be ready for four months more siege, the question of food supplies for natives has become very serious. Two of these unfortunate fugitives were shot last night in their endeavours to elude the vigilance of the cordon all round us. It is not the question of meat so much as the question of grain, which is our difficulty.

11th, Sunday. I was aroused about dawn by musketry fire, and as I heard no more, supposed I had been dreaming, but when starting for my early ride, was told there had been heavy firing to the east. I went to Fort Ayr, from whence the Boer fort seemed ridiculously close, and so on to the Cape Police fort, and from there the Boer sniping station looked within six hundred yards. I was, however, informed that it was a good sixteen hundred yards off. It was a perfectly lovely morning, and had one's horse only felt as fresh as the morning, the ride would have been indeed enjoyable, but the stress of the siege in the way of shortness of provisions has fallen far more severely on the horses than the human beings.

From this fort I rode to the B. Squadron horse lines. The horses are not at present a pleasing spectacle, but, owing to our extended grazing ground, I dare say they could still do some work. Sundry of them are killed and turned into *billtong* for the *kaffirs*. Thence along the picturesque bank of the Molopo, through the centre of the *stadt* to breakfast at Captain Marsh's. This officer, whose squadron has held the *stadt* since the commencement of the siege, has, from his West Coast experiences, a wonderful knack of dealing with natives, and in a great measure the absolute confidence of the Baralongs in the white garrison may be ascribed to him, they have accordingly constituted him a sort of universal referee in all their local troubles. After breakfast we walked out from the edge of the *stadt* to the two forts occupied by Sergeant Abrahams and his detachment of natives, within six hundred yards of which are situated the Boer forts, also garrisoned by natives. Between the opposing forts both sides rambled at their own sweet will.

We then went on to Fort Cronje, originally in the occupation of the Boers, and having attained our utmost limits we sat and smoked and looked at the *stadt* (distant about a mile), and appreciated how Mafeking looked to the Boers from their western outposts. Personally, the northern end of the *stadt* reminds me of nothing so much as the Curragh Camp when viewed from the Newbridge Road, and, indeed, the *veldt* all round looked fresh, green, and undulating enough for the Curragh itself. Fort Cronje is enfiladed by the blockhouse north of the Molopo. Eastward from Sergeant Abrahams' fort, and in a circular direction across the railway line towards Cannon Kopje, extend forts occupied by McKenzie's contingent. We thus now have a large and secure grazing ground, the area of which I had not previously appreciated. We strolled back to the *stadt* and rode back to shop and church.

During the morning and afternoon occurred some of those interchanges of courtesy between ourselves and our opponents, which generally do take place on Sunday. Corporal Currie, who during the week spends all his time in endeavouring to slay and not be slain by the Boers, was called over by them to translate a note they had received. They offered him tobacco and small civilities, and patted him on the back saying he was a *"freundlish kerel."* They also said they were sick of it, and what a waste of time it was not to be ploughing. A somewhat similar conversation was carried on by Mr. Greenfield on the other side. The Dutch, in addition, said they thought it would all be over in a month, that they hadn't got any papers, but would give them to us at the first opportunity, which we understood to mean, when their romancing journalists had sufficiently seasoned the dish of Dutch defeats for Mafeking consumption.

The bicycle sports had to be postponed owing to the condition of the track, but there was a cricket match in the morning between Fitzclarence's squadron and the town of Mafeking, which the latter won by nineteen runs, and in the afternoon a concert, where our commanding officer, as usual, distinguished himself by his comic songs and humorous sketches. This talent is well known to his friends, but is certainly not so well known to the British public, who only have had the advantage of viewing him from a serious side; however, we appreciated him quite as much in his lighter capacity, and the concert was a great success.

The Beleaguered Batchelors' Ball, given by the batchelors of Mafeking, had in consequence of Mr. Call's death been postponed till tonight. It commenced merrily enough, and had been going on for about an hour when history and the Duchess of Richmond's ball repeated itself. The staff officer arrived warning all officers to fall in.

Boers' attack on a R.S.A.P. Fort.

Heavy firing commenced all round, and an attack was anticipated. The galloping Maxim raced across the *veldt* in the dark from the western outposts to the town, at no time a pleasant journey, and now with the innumerable pitfalls all round it, it was lucky to get there without a smash. The Bechuanaland Rifles and a squadron of the Protectorate Regiment were pushed forwards towards the brickfields, taking the place of the Cape Police who had reinforced the extreme eastern advanced posts. The Boers had put three hundred more men into their advance trench and kept up a heavy fire at intervals all night, as indeed they did at all points. Our men did not fire much.

12th. At dawn this morning I went to Ellis's corner, as heavy firing was going on in that direction. The five-pounder was firing at Currie's post and the Cape Police, from the Boer main trench at under two hundred yards. Their quick firer and one-pound Maxim were also doing so. The big gun seemed anxious to participate, and was elevated several times, but owing to the Boer trench being immediately in the line of fire did not venture to. Things slackened somewhat at half-past six, and I went for a ride round the western side where a few odd shots were being fired, but nothing was going on. About half-past eight the big gun commenced firing at Cannon Kopje, and after half a dozen shots transferred her attentions to the town, mainly bursting in fairly close proximity to this dugout, but so far no damage to my knowledge. This afternoon I take up my residence at Cannon Kopje for a bit.

12th. continued. When I had finished the last paragraph I left my dugout and went to lunch, and as I walked to the hotel, heard a single shot, of which I naturally took no notice. An hour afterwards I heard that it had claimed its victim in Captain R. Girdwood, late 3rd Battalion Royal Irish Rifles, assistant commissariat officer here, who was mortally wounded. To the garrison and all who knew him the blow was severe. Throughout the whole siege he was always laughing and joking, and nothing ever subdued his never failing cheerfulness; to meet him was a regular tonic if liver or temper were at fault. The duty he did in assisting Captain Ryan to regulate the supplies of food and stores was invaluable, and Colonel Baden-Powell in his general order literally expressed the great regret and sympathy felt for his wife. In the evening I went up to the *kopje*, and am for a time attached to the B.S.A.P. Prior to my departure they gave us a good doing in the town, both musketry and shell fire.

IN THE TRENCHES.

13th. To sleep in the open and live on the heights in fine weather is undoubtedly an improvement on the town, at any rate for a short time; though one is away from headquarters and the latest garrison gossip, one's view of proceedings is universal and uninterrupted, unless one happens to be the recipient of Boer favours. The bomb proof gives ample cover and a dining-room, for the rest one lives in the open which, in this perfect weather, unless the sun be unduly hot, is charming, and though washing arrangements be scanty, the air is better and the view far less circumscribed than in the town some two thousand yards away. Last night wild musketry fire went on all night, and incendiary Boer shells provided the *kopje* contingent with fireworks *gratis*, and only succeeded in setting one house on fire, which was quickly extinguished. Poor Girdwood died this afternoon and was buried this evening.

14th, Valentine's Day. I rode into the town and having transacted my business, and had a pleasant ride round the western outposts, returned just in time to elude their first shells. They are messing about their works as usual, but what they are doing we cannot quite make out. They have, however, withdrawn their marquees from their gun at McMullan's farm. The homely Dutch families generally play about the gun (the Asp on the Cocktrice's den—N.B. the Cocktrice's business end directed on us), and when family life is most in evidence in the gun's vicinity they generally fire on the town, as it does not amuse the dear things to fire at a small mark where they may possibly do no damage, whilst they think they cannot well miss everybody in the town.

The fair ladies frequently fire the gun themselves and dandle their babies on high to look on at the prospective slaughter of English women and children. Charming race! I think even Sheridan could scarcely find a Dutch woman "an excuse for a glass," or, indeed, an excuse for anything else. However, if their menkind had as much pluck as they possess venom, Mafeking would not now be flying the Union Jack, but the Vierkleur of billous hue. This is plentiful in the vicinity, but has not, and will not, desecrate the township, and I trust the new issue may serve as a model for the ribbon of our Transvaal medal. Sundown: Creaky dismantled. Are they sick of it at last?

15th. As dawn broke a crowd of us went up to the lookout post, to look for our dear departed, and when we failed to find her we accepted our loss with due philosophy. I rode over to Fort Ayr to see Mr.

BOER HORSES DURING ACTION UNDER CREST OF HILL OCCUPIED BY BURGHERS

Greenfield, who is isolated for a month in this post. He must, when not engaged in rallies with the Boers, find it very dull, for he accepted with avidity the offer of my diary of the siege to read. He had, however, found Creaky in front of his position and about five miles due west of the town; what she proposes to do here time will show, but our end is pretty safe from her. Later I received a telephone message to say how pleased he was with the account of the fight of November 31st. This blunder, in my diary, is a legacy from my late typewriter. His last batch of copy (which was the last straw that gave the correspondent the "hump") dated the 12th, though irritating, was rather amusing, I have now transferred my favours elsewhere. The gun has commenced bombarding the *stadt* and women's *laager*.

16th. I rode up to Major Godley's and had the "31st of November" cast in my teeth once more (since corrected). The big gun fired twenty-eight shots at the *stadt* and women's *laager*. From Cannon Kopje there is twenty-three-and-a-half seconds between the smoke from her muzzle and the report, which makes her a matter of nine thousand yards away, and about the same from the centre of the town which she cannot now properly reach, and to strike which at all, she is elevated apparently at right angles. She devoted several shells to McKenzie's western shelter trenches, doing no harm, however. Her change of position must have been another deliberate atrocity on the part of the Boers, for which I trust their commander will be strictly called to account.

There can be no immediate effect expected on the defences or ultimate resistance of Mafeking by the deliberate bombardment of women and children, black or white. And he who sows the storm may reap the whirlwind, for the blacks neither forget nor forgive, and this is one more, and by no means the least, tally in a long score. Now, as regards the position of the Baralongs and our other native residents.

At the outbreak of the war, the Boers flooded the town with all the refugee *kaffirs* from Johannesburg and other parts of the Transvaal, who happened to be in our vicinity, hoping either on the capture of the town, which they confidently anticipated, to secure a good labour market, or, in the event of an unexpectedly protracted resistance, to exercise through these additional mouths, a severe pressure on our food supplies, and thus indirectly on our length of defence. They carefully, however, first robbed them of all their money. Now, picking a *kaffir's* pocket, or wherever he may carry his money, ranks about as high in the code of honour, as stealing coppers from a blind man's plate. I am not sure whether it is a transgression of the Law of Nations, but as by the time this diary is read the Boer will not be, as he certainly never ought to have been, a nation, it is of small moment, but the act of robbery distinctly took place. The Baralongs were assured by both sides that the war was between two white races, and that they had no cause to interfere. We went even further, and refused to allow them to assist us.

However, when the Baralong had seen his cattle raided, his *kraals* burnt, and himself bombarded, he, somewhat of a rhetorician, but lacking perhaps in the logical capacity for distinguishing between "a military operation" and "an act of war," decided that the Boers' application of the former to his property was good enough excuse for him to indulge in the latter to prevent a further application, he accordingly, in his childlike manner, invited the Boers to enter his *stadt*, and shot several of them when they tried to. Recently, too, the Boers made overtures to secure the Baralong assistance, and the Chief, Wessels, said he must think it over; after long deliberation he declined. It was probably in order to punish them for this lack of readiness to support them, that the Boers so slated the *stadt*. However this may be, the Baralongs and other natives have loyally and consistently supported us, and deserve ample compensation for the hardships, privations, and losses which they have sustained.

All day the Boers have been making feeble attempts on McKenzie's outpost; and at night, seated at the *kopje*, one could see a circle of fire running all round the outposts. On the eastern side, our Maxim in the brickfields, our seven-pounder and their five-pounder and many rifles were flashing in the darkness; in the distance Fort Ayr was warmly engaged, while to support McKenzie in our immediate proximity, the armoured train was creaking and groaning up the grass-grown line. And nothing perhaps brings home our isolation so much, as to see the rails overgrown with grass, and reflect that this is a main line to England. Owing to the custom of the Boer of elevating the muzzle of his rifle over the parapet and firing in the air, bullets were whistling and falling all round us on the *kopje* all night, which, as we were a mile from, and two hundred feet higher than, the trench they were firing at, argued poor marksmanship on their part. However, we were all fairly safe, and the Boer presumably quite so, and as he made plenty of noise I suppose everybody was satisfied.

17th. Very little firing till the evening, and then usual performance.

18th, Sunday. Our usual quiet day. The bank now opens for business on Sundays. As the *kaffirs*, in common with other natives, persist in burying their specie, it is very literally locked up, and to restore the circulation of silver we have a paper issue for small sums. Indeed, we are now a very self-contained community, we have our bank, our ordnance factory, our police, and flourish under a beneficent and remote autocracy. As regards the ordnance, the factory was started for the manufacture of shells for our seven-pounders, for shot, brass and iron, for our antique cannon, and for the adaptation of five-pounder shells (left here by Dr. Jameson) to our seven-pounders by the addition of enlarged driving bands; these have all proved a complete success, and too much praise cannot be given to Connely and Cloughlan of the Locomotive Department, who have organized and run the aforesaid factory. As great a triumph has been the manufacture of powder, and invention of fuses by Lieutenant Daniel, B.S.A.P., and Glamorgan Artillery Militia, and thus we are rendered secure against our ammunition running short; a gun is also being manufactured, and will shortly be used. This factory is of long standing, but prior to this the authorities have not allowed us to allude to its existence.

19th. Went out to try and shoot plover, which form an acceptable addition to our rations, as we have now come down to horse-flesh and six ounces of bread per day. Fairly quiet day. Strolling down to town in the evening, I assumed that their snipers were too much occupied with our people in the brickfields to bother about me. They were not, however, and were unpleasantly attentive.

20th. Retransferred my residence to the town, the firing is heavier down here through the day, and also, indeed, the night, but here we are under cover.

21st. Gun did not fire more than two or three shots, but at night there was very heavy firing along the brickfield front, they shot some of the working party, and also headed some of the natives going towards Kanya. The Boers made a half-hearted sort of attempt to turn our men out of the advanced trench, but utterly failed. The question of feeding the natives has been solved by the establishment of a soup kitchen, the component parts of the stock may be varied, but the result is eminently nutritious.

Gun changed back near to old position east of town, they elevated and depressed her several times, but did not fire. As the bells rung, however, the moral effect was exactly the same, possibly also the physical. Sergeant-Major Looney, A.S.C., was reduced to the ranks and five years penal servitude awarded to him for selling government stores. Private Miller, Protectorate Regiment, tampering with a loaded ninety-four-pound shell, was blown to pieces. This form of lunacy is apparently ineradicable. We anticipate an attack tomorrow, as it is the Orange Free State Independence Day. I wonder if the Free State still exists: the following letter *apropos* of this from the leader of the opposition in the Free State before the war is, I think, interesting:—

(*Copy.*)

Blomfontein,
September 4th, 1899.

Charles Mettam, Esq.,
Box 23.
Krugersdorp.
Dear Mr. Mettam,
Your letter of the 30th inst. is to hand, and affords a by no means solitary instance of the one sided and high-handed treatment former Free State *Burghers* have to undergo at the hands of our so-called brethren in the South African Republic, yet in spite of all this the political union or alliance was put through our Raad, and should hostilities break out, we shall have to be belligerents and be involved in all the horrors of war and have to lose our independence, and for what? As a just reward for the folly of allowing a spurious sentiment to override common sense. So it is, however—and under the circumstances, as you have lost your Free State *burgher* rights you could not claim protection here. The only way I see for you—as you hold to your birthright staters—is to bring your position to the notice of the British resident, and ask him to advise you how you are to act. With kindest regards to Mrs. Mettam and yourself.
Yours faithfully,

J. G. Fraser.
P.S.—I think a great many of our people are being educated by this crisis to the accuracy of the policy which I placed before them at the last election, and have since always advocated.

J.G.F.

Sir,

I beg to acknowledge receipt of your letter and enclosure (herewith returned) of the 7th instant, and regret that it is not in my power to discuss the matter to which you refer by letter. I should, however, recommend you, if you should be in Johannesburg, to see the British Vice-Consul there, who will no doubt give you such advice as may be possible under the circumstances.

I am, Sir,

Your obedient servant,

Conyngham Greene.

Mr. C. Mettam,
P. O. Box 23,
Krugersdorp.
Certified true copy.
E. H. Cecil Maj,
C. S. O.

23rd. They commenced shelling cattle and northern end of the town. As the inhabitants have not been shelled severely for ten days, they seem more concerned in running to see where the shell pitches, than in taking cover as they have been strictly warned to do. Steady rain has commenced, depressing the big gun and the Boers.

24th. Rain continuing, gun and owners still depressed. No news received for ten days and great universal anxiety felt for anticipated decisive intelligence.

25th, Sunday. No heavy shelling yesterday, but firing all night and this morning. Cape Boys in advanced trenches, and Boers, engaged in an argument as to their respective mothers and other female relatives' merits and demerits. The arguments for and against having rapidly degenerated to assertions, shooting began, but as it was merely a personal quarrel no one else interfered, and, indeed, white flags from both sides met within a quarter of a mile of the firing, which continued all day. Our Sunday concert was a great success, and the day being fine was most enjoyable.

It is curious what different people buy at the stores, the Europeans buying mainly the necessities of life, while the *kaffir*, who has plenty of money, but is only allowed to purchase a limited amount of meal, browses off *Pâte de Foie Gras*, and other similar comestibles. In the afternoon I went to inspect our new gun. She reflects the greatest credit on her builders, the finish and turn-out being quite dandy. She's a smooth bore 5.5, and carries a round shell; we ought to have good fun from her.

26th. Runners in this morning, news very meagre. Her Majesty's telegram received, which gave intense satisfaction, but we have been anxiously anticipating decisive intelligence. The *kaffirs* report that the Boers are few round here, but will not abandon the prosecution of the siege; on our side we cannot afford a serious sortie, as a reverse *might* mean the fall of Mafeking, which is not desirable or in the least probable. The Boers began shell-fire at dawn this morning, and continued it at intervals all day. This was the most rapid fire we have had, and the continuous clanging of bells might have induced a stranger to suppose that we were indulging in some popular celebration. They particularly favoured our end of the town. In the evening we tried our new gun on Game Tree Fort at about 2300 yards, she was a great success, and her range was apparently only limited by eyesight.

27th. Being Majuba Day we expected an attack, so I went up to Cannon Kopje before dawn. What attacking there was was in the brickfields and was done by us, but after a fitful splutter of musketry for an hour things quieted down. I went up to Fort Ayr but nothing was doing, and with the exception of musketry fire and a few small shells, it was a quiet day. The Boers blew up the line about two miles north of the town.

28th. We have got our news at last, and though the shell fire is very much heavier than usual the population is wandering about with a bland smile on its face and a comfortable contempt for the Boer nation at large, only tempered by the fear that the military success over Boer armies in the field may be discounted greatly if the British people allow themselves to be hoodwinked by the most unscrupulous, self-interested politicians who ever led a country to its ruin, but who have unfortunately sown seeds which may sprout again and to which there is only one successful treatment, that of *force majeure*, followed by *pax Brittanica*, to be upheld again whenever necessary by the aforesaid *force majeure*, which is the only argument that South Africa, black or white, in its present condition can understand. Generosity would be wasted, kindness treated with ill-concealed contempt, and blood and treasure cast away, whilst race hatred would again be rampant, were the Dutch to be once more in a position to struggle for supreme control. It is a strong man armed who keeps South Africa, let that man be British.

The Boers are determined to keep us amused, and do not approve of the Free Press; they have just now blown the newspaper office, by our dug-out, to pieces, and are trying to silence our mild manifestations of joy by particularly heavy shell fire. This afternoon we tried our new gun again on the *veldt*, with bursting charges in the shells, and the results were eminently satisfactory; they afforded a certain amount of interest to the garrison of Game Tree fort, who, as the gun was pointed almost at right angles to them, bobbed somewhat unnecessarily to each discharge. The explosion of the shell might well have puzzled them for it was exactly like the discharge of another gun.

It is a shame to be cooped up here in such weather, "where all around is beautiful and only Boers are vile," and if they had any sense of decency or humour they would give us one good fight to finish, as it is we hang on in trenches into which they cannot possibly come, they hang on in opposing trenches into which we cannot afford to go, exchanges of shots go on all day, varied by shell fire on their part, which is becoming monotonous, and the dullest, deadest level of warfare has been effectually attained.

Today we had our little joke; a dummy truck was placed on the line about two miles south of the town, some snipers fired a few shots from it and then abandoned it, they were, however, successful in drawing the fire from the quick-firer Krupp and one-pound Maxim at Jackal Tree with occasional shots from the big gun; they made execrable shooting, but killed some cattle and a horse or two in a remote portion of the *veldt*, and unfortunately killed the Sergeant-Major of the Black Watch, a fine Zulu over six feet four inches: a one-pound Maxim hit him clean in the head. Yesterday, too, Trooper Elkington, a particularly smart, good-looking fellow in the Cape Police, was struck in the face by a five-pound shell, and his nose and eyes destroyed; he still lives, poor fellow.

Apropos of Zulus, there is a mad Zulu in the town who, when the frenzy seizes him, strips, and indulges in a war dance in front of the Boers; how many thousand rounds of ammunition they have fired at him it would be hard to say, but one day for certain they fired a five nine-pounder Krupp at him, the only result being that he *assegaied* the spot were each shell fell. My own personal experience of him was aggravating. One day having selected a secluded spot with good cover from which to snipe, and thinking myself exceedingly well concealed, I was much annoyed by the inordinate amount of bullets which came my way, and whilst waiting till they stopped a bit, happened to look round and discovered that my friend, stark naked, was dancing about a hundred yards in rear of me, when he had finished he put on his clothes and went home. He is still alive, (as at time of first publication), and dancing when inclined.

Mr. Whales, who has edited *The Mafeking Mail* and brought out daily editions throughout the siege, had an extraordinary escape yesterday. A 94 lb. shell came into his office and exploded whilst he was talking to two other men, wrecking the place, but providentially only slightly scratching one man. As he emerged from the *debris* much shaken, his first remark was, "That the slip would not be issued tonight." This is the second shell through the office, and though the setting up operations are carried on in a bomb proof, he has consistently carried on his editorial avocations regardless of the heaviest fire.

This practice I am glad to say he proposes to discontinue in a measure, and work more or less underground, for, as he truly says, "The third shell may hit me." Really this does look as if it were the beginning of the end, and as if this somewhat isolated outpost of the empire were going to get its communications with civilization restored. It has been an experience, and though certainly not a very pleasant one, I do not think the survivors can but have profited by it. I rather fancy, however, that it will take a singularly astute foeman ever to involve any of them in a siege again; it is, however, Colonel Vyvyan's second experience in South Africa, as he was once before shut up in Etchowe.

March 1st. Yesterday a large party of women and children, who do not belong to this district, were sent away; the Boers turned them back, and when they were retiring deliberately opened a heavy fire on them, killing and wounding many. This is not the first deliberate outrage on the native women and children, and in addition they have flogged and turned back women trying to escape. Colonel Baden-Powell has addressed several remonstrances to General Snyman on the subject, and pointed out that he cannot expect the native chiefs in the vicinity to restrain their tribesmen, if the Boers persist in murdering their friends and relations, and that he, Colonel Baden-Powell, cannot be answerable for any subsequent occurrences in the way of reprisals on the part of the natives, to which General Snyman has answered as a rule more or less civilly (generally less) that we and the natives may do our worst.

Today is the usual sort of day, heavy sniping at intervals and a fair amount of shelling. Certainly the amount of damage done to Mafeking in life and property has been wholly disproportionate to the amount of shell fire sustained, the reason of course being the soft mud bricks of which the houses are constructed; and today we had two very fine object lessons of the extensive damage these shells would have done among more solidly constructed edifices. Mr. Whitely, the mayor's, house, which is built of stronger materials than any other house in Mafeking, was struck by a shell, and the damage done was far greater than was usually the case.

Round the house of Mr. Bell, the magistrate, there is a loose stone wall, the shell struck and exploded at the base of it, the fragments of shell did but little harm, but one boulder about twice the size of a man's body was hurled about twenty-five yards, and two rocks about twice the size of a man's head were projected through the house some twenty-five yards away, while stones of various sizes were hurled great distances and in every direction. So, though thanks to its flimsy construction, Mafeking has escaped better than many a more important town would, it does seem rather like breaking a butterfly to use modern siege guns against a place of this sort. However, it is still a fairly lively butterfly in spite of twelve thousand pounds of metal from one gun alone. We have developed a new trench N.E. of the town to enfilade the enemies' sniping trenches, which, though it does not silence them, seems to annoy them passably.

2nd. Shell fire. Our new gun was tried on the sniping trenches, more for ranging purposes and to learn her extent and powers than anything else. The Boer trenches showed great curiosity as to what she was and why she did it, for her shells burst with a most delightful report and seemed to spread very nicely. A new toy like this is a godsend to us in our present dull condition.

The Boers during the experiment, however, kept themselves and their curiosity underground. The Boer big gun was removed at sunset and the usual crop of surmises, bets as to destination, cause of removal, &c., sprang rapidly into existence, and at any rate gave us something to talk about; it takes very little to interest us here.

3rd. The Boers tried dynamiting our trenches last night, but failed, our advanced parties are within forty yards of each other. At dawn the big gun, which had shifted back to the south-east heights from where she flanks our brickfield advance, commenced heavy fire, sending thirty-six or thirty-eight shells before breakfast, and mortally wounding Sergeant-Major Taylor of the Cape Boys; we also had four or five others wounded more or less severely. They, however, stuck to their ground in shallow trenches which were hardly any protection, and that we suffered no greater loss is a matter of astonishment to everybody.

Our seven-pounders then commenced on their trenches, and the firing was heavy all round the whole morning. The Boers contemplated renewing their entertainment in the afternoon, but our snipers had crept up to within about eight hundred yards of the big gun and commenced picking off the gunners. Trooper Webb, C.P., fortunately shot their artillery officer whilst laying the gun, at a fairly early stage in the performance, and this seemed to damp their enthusiasm. They commenced running about like a lot of disturbed ants, messengers were dispatched to the laager, their doctor arrived on horseback, and they then proceeded to hoist three Red Cross flags on the work. They carried a stretcher under a guard towards the *laager* and met a carriage, but he was apparently too bad to be put in that, and the carriage returned to the laager, when some mounted men rode forth, and, meeting the stretcher, dismounted and followed behind. Altogether they seemed very depressed whilst we were correspondingly the reverse, and in the confusion the big gun forgot to go off, and was removed before dark. With the exception of musketry the rest of the day was quiet. Our saps have now crossed each other.

Sunday. This morning at daybreak the Boers were still working, so we gave them a volley at forty yards and are believed to have shot four. Sniping continued all day, and later on we killed another. From this quarter the Boers, who were evidently very cross, sniped viciously all day. I walked up with Captain Williams, whose turn it is now for duty in the brickfields, and personally I consider it a most undesirable place of residence. The big gun has disappeared. We are all glad to hear that our old friend Cronje is in a tight place; from all accounts he will trouble us no more.

5th. The big gun is back at the old place east of the town; her immediate *entourage* evidently prefer gun practice at a safe range, for we have shot a good many gunners. Their efforts to get the gun off under musketry fire always cause amusement. They rush to the gun, and then disappear, this goes on sometimes quite a long time before the gun gets fired. Sergeant Major Taylor died last night; he was a splendid fellow and a good representative of the Cape Boys, who are a most gallant race of men and good shots. In times of peace he was one of the leading members of the Church in the location. There is heavy firing in the direction of the brickfields, so I must see what is going on.

6th. Yesterday our seven-pounders made very good shooting on the Boer brickfield trenches, and after Mr. Feltham, Protectorate Regiment, had thrown dynamite at them for some time, the Cape Boys went to poke them out of their sap with the bayonet, but the wily Boer was gone; they had closed their sap. In this fight of "sit down" (as the Zulus say), I for one had worn out much patience and several pairs of trousers, and we seem to be borrowing more and more hints in the way of mortars, hand grenades, &c., from our forefathers. The Boers seemed much annoyed yesterday afternoon, and heavy firing went on last night and is going on this morning. The big gun did not fire yesterday though she was elevated and pointed several times, nor has she fired this morning. There are strong rumours that the Boers intend to trek, and are preparing for it; that the gun we see is a dummy; and that the real one has been withdrawn to defend a position on the frontier. We sincerely hope it is true.

6th. The gun proved herself to be the "old original" by letting us have two or three shots in the evening.

7th. Heavy firing all night in the brickfields; only two shells. The Boers have commenced to *trek*. Trooper McDonald, Cape Police, died. His was an adventurous career; he joined the Argyle and Sutherland Highlanders in '47, served in the Crimea (French and Sardinian Medal, two clasps), served in the Indian Mutiny, was kidnapped when embarking home by Americans, fought for the North against the South, deserted the North and fought for the South, afterwards went to Australia, thence to New Zealand, and served in the Maori War where he was taken prisoner. Later he came to South Africa, served in the Basuto War, Sir Charles Warren's expedition, Carrington's Horse, the B.B.P., and transferred to the Cape Police, in which corps he has died of hardships and old age, fighting the Boers. He is not the only Crimean veteran we have here, both the navy and army are represented.

Mr. Ellis joined the Royal Navy in 1854, served in the Baltic and the Black Sea, came to Africa and served in the Galika War. Mr. Brasier served in the Crimea and Mutiny, and there are others of whose extent of service I am not so certain. The contrast between them and the Cadet Corps, who are utilised for orderly work, &c., is remarkable, and if the Boers have their greybeards and boys fighting, why so have we.

It seems very curious at first, but one soon gets used to it, as indeed one does to the underground residences, all business, as far as possible, being carried on in dug-outs; dining-rooms, offices, stores, barracks, even the bank where Mr. Urry, who with Captain Greener runs our paper coinage, sits in charge of a vast amount of paper, but very little hard cash, for the *kaffirs* have buried all specie obtainable, are below ground.

In our dugout we have some siege mice, born since its construction, of a friendly and confiding disposition, who come and feed on the table, and play about and have a good time generally; other animals are therefore not admitted.

8th. Good news arrived of Cronje's defeat and surrender, and the wiping out of Majuba Day. Soldiers were proud, the population at large delighted, but most of all the South African Englishman. For the last twenty years he has been taunted by the Dutch with Majuba; he can now hold up his head again, and nothing could conduce more to a permanent pacification of South Africa than the wiping out of the day. Henning Pretorius, one of the leading Transvaal *burghers*, when he heard of Majuba, said, "Now it is finished. They will never stop till they have wiped us out." This he maintained till his death, which occurred recently, and he always urged that the Boers should make friends with us and become one nation. Usual heavy firing at night, only one shell.

9th. Heavy firing all night, commencing early with heavy volleys on the north and north-west fronts. I rode round the western outposts; it is a very pleasant ride and the Boers were pretty quiet, at least as concerned me, for they took no notice at all.

10th. Heavy firing this morning in the brickfields, the gun is elevated and pointed on the town, in which position she has remained for the past two or three days with very occasional shells. The Boers are daily *treking* by degrees. I propose to go down to the brickfields this morning as that is about the liveliest spot in Mafeking, though I fancy very little of it will go a long way.

Trooper Webb of the Cape Police was shot through the head in the brickfield trenches last night; a fine specimen of a splendid corps.

He was shot through the ankle in a sortie at the commencement of the siege, and when able to hobble he came out for duty as look-out man and orderly at headquarters; yesterday, as he was not so lame, at his earnest request he was allowed to go on duty in the advanced trenches, and during his first tour of sentry-go, was mortally wounded by a chance bullet in the dark. He is greatly regretted by the towns-people and all ranks, and Her Majesty loses a fine soldier, a first-class policeman, and a good all-round man.

I went down to the brickfields this morning and met Captain Fitz-clarence and Captain Williams; things were pretty quiet down there in the morning, though they livened up again shortly afterwards. I went round the trenches with them. One's mode of progression is distinctly uncomfortable, bent double, with a certain amount of water in the trenches, which are shallow as yet between the various works, but being deepened daily. The various works and trenches all have their names, Regent's Circus, Oxford Street, &c., whilst our most advanced work is called the New Cut, and the Boers' trench forty yards away Houndsditch. The sound of the Mauser at this short range has a very different effect to its sound at the longer ranges, and the crack of the bullets when they strike is like the explosion of a young shell.

The Boers at these ranges are very quick and good shots; they shoot at your hat if visible, or at the sound of your voice, and as the loopholes have to be kept closed, the only way of looking out is by means of a pair of Zeiss glasses which project over the edge of the parapet while one's head is in safety some inches below, even so they put a bullet through one of the lenses this morning (which, as they were mine, did not please me) and through the hat of the look-out man, but with them you can see right into the Boer loopholes with comparative safety, though bullets frequently, owing to the tremendous penetration of the Mauser, come clean through the upper part of the parapet, and the sand bags on the top are cut to ribbons.

The advance post is occupied by the Cape Boys, who under Lieutenants Feltham and Currie (who has recently been promoted) take it day and day about; one was shot this morning. This post which we now occupy was sapped up to and occupied from the other side by the Boers, but was retaken by the Cape Boys under Currie, with Captain Fitzclarence and some of the white garrison; they had to emerge in single file from a narrow opening which was commanded by the Boer loop-holes, and run round the edge of the excavation of the brickfield up to the loop-holes occupied by the Boers, a distance of some twenty yards; the latter fled on their approach.

We have now occupied it from our side and strengthened the work. The trenches approaching the advance works are exposed to fire from the front and right flanks, but are being strengthened daily. On our return from the advance work we made our way to the river bed where Currie's post is established, and it was there that poor Webb was killed. The garrison of the trenches are now fairly housed and comparatively safe, though, of course, casualties occur daily; still, if the Boers try a sortie they will meet a very warm reception.

Sunday. Last night heavy firing as usual, but today, contrary to our late custom, peace has reigned in the brickfields, and both sides sat on their parapets and asked after various friends on the other side. The Boers have lately, as the natives express it, become much more tame, and have allowed *kaffir* women to gather wood, pumpkins, and *kaffir* corn without molestation. Our Sunday was absolutely peaceful and quiet, and as we are not able now to indulge in mounted sports, &c., owing to the condition of the horses, we have fallen back on cricket as our Sunday relaxation.

12th. The natives went out last night, and McKenzie's boys got into Jackal Tree which they found empty. The Baralongs attacked Fort Snyman from the rear and had a lively engagement with the hundred odd Boers who garrisoned it, and after finishing their ammunition, withdrew with a loss of one killed and two wounded. We know of one Boer dead for certain, for Trooper Webb of the C.P. blew his head off at the entrance to the work, and we fancy that at the short range our volleys must have accounted for several more. General Snyman has returned and notified his arrival by an unusually heavy dose of shell fire. I rode round the western outposts this morning with Captain Wilson; the natives seemed quite pleased with themselves, more particularly as they had secured some thirty head of fat cattle in a raid two days ago. We then inspected the soup kitchens which he is managing, and which are a great improvement on those first started; the food provided is very popular with the natives, who come in their hundreds for it.

13th. Our runners brought us in good news of the relief of Ladysmith and the heavy Boer losses. Everybody is consequently jubilant, and our only regret is that we can't drive these Boers over the frontier and clear British territory; however, Colonel Plumer is at Lobatsi, and as there cannot be any considerable body of Boers between this and

Kimberley, we ought soon to have the line open both ways. They began shelling early and kept on with their home-made shrapnel all day, killing two and wounding several. One shell burst in a pigeon-house and killed sixteen valuable carrier pigeons; the shot is somewhat large for pigeon shooting, but apparently effective.

The base of another shell went through the headquarter office, making a hideous mess, but hurting no one; in fact, they were shooting offices all round, and the ordinarily neatly-kept official papers were in two or three cases much upset and covered with the *debris* of their various abodes. This new shrapnel is essentially a man-killing shell, for which reason I suppose the Boers have paid particular attention to the earthworks, *per contra* if they want to snipe cattle or slay men they generally employ common shell. Last night a cattle raiding party came in with some horses, saddles, rifles and bandoliers belonging to some deceased Boers.

The Boers had tracked this party of Baralongs, who, seeing them following on their spoor, had doubled back on their own trail and ambushed them at short range. They accounted for six or seven, and relieved their dead of their arms, &c., as far as they could, before the Boers recovered from their surprise, and drove them off with a loss to the raiders of one killed and two wounded, the latter of whom they brought in. This success has naturally much pleased the natives, and encouraged them greatly for future raids, which is most useful, as the results feed us and harass the Boers. The advanced trenches also got a couple by moonlight as they were creeping up to our trench.

14th. Shelling has begun again this morning, quite up to its best form. The Boers in Snyman's absence take things much more easily, and if we could only kill him here and Kruger in the south, as well as old Cronje, it would save a vast amount of trouble, for it takes these leaders all their time to keep their followers up to the scratch. They had a sort of "*indaba*" this morning. I only trust it was bad news for them, they get their news about a fortnight before we do.

15th. Fairly quiet day, pretty heavy shelling.

16th. Very little shelling. The Cape Boys in the advance trenches were playing a concertina, and so chaffed the Boers, saying they were dancing, and asking them to send some ladies, &c., that one of them, either attracted by the music or bursting with *repartee*, popped up his head, and was incontinently shot by a wily Cape Boy, to the intense delight of the others. They have a distinct sense of humour, though possibly a somewhat grim one. The advance trenches are now deepened and strengthened, and are as safe as it is possible for them to be to walk about in; from the advance trenches the Boers and ourselves throw bombs, and they are also using explosive bullets; their bombs are made like old hand-grenades, the bombs of both sides being charged with dynamite. They throw theirs by hand, but ours, though of a cruder form (being mainly jam tins) are propelled in a much more scientific manner. Sergeant Page, of the Protectorate Regiment, has rigged up a bamboo as a fishing-rod, and casts his bomb with great precision the short distance to the Boer trenches.

17th. Pretty quiet day. Last night McKenzie's boys raided Jackal Tree Fort, killed one Boer and a *kaffir*, and secured three horses and rifles. The dugouts are all so close to various residences that it was amusing to see one card party, disturbed by the ringing of the bell, dive from the mess to the dugout, and actually be back picking up their cards before the shell which had passed high in the air, had exploded. Vices in time of peace become virtues in war time; the most expert Baralong cattle thief, who under other circumstances would assuredly be in durance vile, is now indeed a *persona grata* and leader of men, and whilst enjoying himself at the top of his bent is making the most of his fleeting opportunity.

18th, Sunday. I went down to the brickfields to the advanced trenches; down there both parties had agreed not to shoot, and exchanged tobacco for peach brandy, &c., asking after their various friends and relations. I got three snap shots at the Boers in the advance trench, and we studied each other with great curiosity, our clean shirts, collars, and Sunday clothes apparently astonishing them as much as their remarkable grime surprised us. On the way back there is a pleasant meadow, in which we lay and smoked and tried to pretend it was England, though that was somewhat a failure. Whilst down there I met an old warrior who had drifted a long way from his last fight. A native of Bagdad, he was in Sarif (?) Pasha's command at Plevna, which he said was a very different siege to this; he says they fought only occasionally there, and then killed thousands of men, but rested in between, whilst here we were continually shooting.

If we killed thousands here the siege would soon come to an end. The old man is very fit and seems to enjoy his fighting still. Runners came in from the south this morning who had seen the relief of Kimberley, which impressed them very much. They said that the man who wrote the Bible must have been referring to the English army, when he spoke of the Tribes of Israel and the thousands which composed them, and that the aforesaid army was big enough to eat up all the *kaffirs*; they reported, also, that the searchlights of the force advancing up the line had been seen as far as Taungs, and that the Boers were concentrating, but are pretty thick between here and the advancing force.

As regards this place the boot will soon be on the other leg, as the Boers are now afraid to move about except in large bodies, and we hope that our communication will soon be thoroughly restored. The runners from Setlagoli reported that the raiding party I spoke of on the 13th, had killed and wounded some twenty Boers, including the man who had shot one of our Baralongs in cold blood the day before. There was a smoking concert tonight to celebrate St. Patrick's Day, largely attended by Irishmen and others; the proceedings were harmonious throughout.

19th. A fair amount of shelling. A party of Boers and three guns have returned from the north, where native rumour says they have had a repulse, and in which direction musketry fire was faintly heard yesterday morning.

20th. We got runners in from the north; the Boers seem in a bad way all round.

21st. More runners in. Today we were unlucky, and we had a few casualties.

22nd. More runners. Plumer's column twenty-four miles away.

23rd. We shelled the brickfield trench, but did not succeed in drawing fire from the big gun, which has been almost silent for the last few days. In the garrison there are soldiers from all parts of the world, one German veteran who served all through the Franco-German War in the 84th Regiment, Trooper Block by name, was through the Orleans campaign, and has since served in all the South African wars; there are men who served in the Chilian war, the Carlist, and in fact practically every known war for the last fifty years.

24th. Last night the Boers evacuated their brickfield trenches, which we occupied with much cheering; they left several cases of dynamite behind connected with a wire, with which they proposed to blow up our men; the wire was, however, promptly disconnected. In Dutch newspapers discovered in the trenches was found the account of the fall of Bloemfontein, which was confirmed by runners from Plumer this morning. The Boers have now withdrawn to a respectful distance all round the town, which is, however, still invested, but the big gun so far is quiet. This must be the beginning of the end, and we have nearly completed our six months' siege. I fully expect the big gun to be removed in a day or two; last night was the first time she has failed to reply to our artillery fire.

We have started a post-office here, with stamps, &c., and also a very tastefully designed £1 note. I must finish off my entries as a go of fever makes it difficult, almost impossible, to write at all.

24th. Last night Sub-Inspector Murray and Trooper Melahue, Cape Police, went out, and having reconnoitred the rear of the enemy's trench, came to the conclusion that it was unoccupied. Inspector Browne, of the Cape Police, and the Cape Boys under Lieutenants Feltham and Currie, proceeded to occupy it. The Boers had left a mine of 250 lbs. of nitro-glycerine behind. Sergeant Page, Protectorate Regiment, discovered and disconnected the wire. The men cheered themselves hoarse, and rightly too, for this is the most decisive success we have scored since the commencement of the campaign, as the town is now for the first time free from musketry fire, and our guns are again within striking distance of the Boer artillery.

25th, Sunday. The Siege Exhibition took place today. A most creditable exhibition from the ingenuity shown, and also considering its peculiar surroundings. We shall hope to forward some of our exhibits home. I went out and inspected the Boer trench. If it is "*an ill bird that fouls its own nest,*" a Boer is indeed ill. They are occupying a trench about seven hundred yards away, from which they shoot with a certain amount of precision, but with no result, upon their late happy home. Personally, I particularly wished to inspect the brick kilns, at which I had discharged some hundred rounds of ammunition. It is very interesting, but still somewhat annoying to find that it is practically bullet proof; however, on the other hand, the particular place of resort from which I had fired the said ammunition was also fairly safe, so perhaps I had no reason to grumble, and at any rate I had frequently silenced them.

26th, Monday. Exceptionally quiet today. Late at night I was in Mr. Weil's dugout when he received the news of the English troops' arrival at Vryburg. Mafeking accordingly jubilant.[1]

---

1. This eventually turned out to be untrue.

MAFEKING SIEGE NOTE

27th, Tuesday. The Boers commenced early and continued a heavy shell fire all day, pouring more shells into the town than they had any two days of the siege. It was very curious, but the news received the night before caused the population to show more absolute disregard for the shell fire than they had done on many days when the bombardment was comparatively light. The Premier's message to the two Presidents was published this evening, and now even the most pessimistic admit it is possible that there may be a satisfactory solution of the war. We hope we may be able to slightly assist in a less passive manner than heretofore.

28th, Wednesday. After our treat of yesterday, absolute quiet reigns today. Really there is no understanding the Boers. Our locally manufactured field-piece burst last night, but the shell managed to reach the Boer *laager.* What they contemplate and what is their plan of campaign leaves everybody wondering. No ulterior object can be obtained by their desultory mode of conducting operations. Occasional casualties, which is apparently their only object, is the sole result arrived at, and these casualties are, we think, more heavy on their side than ours.

29th, Thursday. A quiet day. The Boers gradually evacuating their eastern trenches.

30th, Friday. The guns are fairly quiet. We are gradually occupying the evacuated trenches.

31st, Saturday. In the morning a quiet day. In the afternoon a body of four hundred or five hundred Boers and three guns hastily left their eastern *laager* in a northerly direction. I took up a position in the convent, and from there could see considerable confusion and excitement amongst the Boers galloping backwards and forwards in the direction of Signal Hill. The sound of guns too was distinctly audible to the north, some six or seven miles away. The garrison livened up. The guns under Major Panzera and Lieutenant Daniells commenced playing from every face. A mounted squadron under Major Grodley demonstrated towards Game Tree fort on the north. For an hour or so things were lively, but quieted down.

Our old "Lord Nelson" reached the *laager*, and the big gun was annoyed by the Hotchkiss. It is a curious fact that all the pieces of ordnance with which we are "blessed" are obsolete naval guns. Rumours as usual flying around and we really had something to give scope for conjecture.

April 1st, Sunday. The siege as affecting me pecuniarily is becoming expensive. I lose bets at the end of each month as it interminably prolongs.

A quiet day and a flag of truce from the Boers asking us to fetch our dead who were killed in the northern fight the day before. Accordingly wagons under Lieutenant the Honourable Hanbury Tracy and Lieutenant Singleton went north, where they met the Boers, who assisted them to find and recover the bodies. Three men were brought in belonging to Colonel Plumer's column, and Captain McLaren, Lieutenant Crewe, and Troopers Murray and Robinson were reported wounded. It would seem to have been a sharp skirmish between a strong patrol of Colonel Plumer's and a considerably more numerous body of Boers, but as far as we can ascertain Colonel Plumer's main column was not engaged.

Our demonstration against Game Tree resulted in our killing two Boers, and even by their own accounts, numerically our losses were evenly balanced. Fourteen dead horses were seen on the field.

2nd, Monday. Flags of truce from the enemy reporting the death of Captain McLaren. Regret and sympathy barely express my own feelings, and how many of us are there scattered about the world, who when they see the next polo tournament, will think again of the best of players, the nicest of fellows, whom Hurlingham and the scenes of his many triumphs will see no more.

There seems a chance of another fight this afternoon. The Boers are very restless and galloping about in all directions. I do not suppose they mean to attack us, and, as far as I can make out, are nervous and seem to expect pressure from the east.

Some men were interviewed yesterday who had returned from Natal. They reported the death of Joubert and were far less confident than they have shown themselves heretofore.

3rd, Tuesday. I am heartily glad to say that Captain McLaren is not dead, although severely wounded and a prisoner in the Boers' hands.

A despatch was received from Colonel Plumer this morning stating that he had had an engagement north of the town and that his losses were Captain Crewe (who was buried here this morning), Lieutenant Milligan, killed; Colonel Plumer, Major Weston Jarvis, and Captain Rolt, slightly wounded; non-commissioned officers and men killed, seven; wounded, twenty-six; missing, eleven. Three missing are known to be dead and the others are wounded in the Boers' hands. Captain

McLaren has written from the Boer camp, where he is, we are all glad to hear, going on well and being very well treated by the Boers.

Yesterday afternoon we had a successful brush with the enemy to north-west, no casualties on our side. Their ambulances were seen very busy. Today everything is so far quiet.

4th. Early this morning Lieutenant F. Smitheman, Rhodesian Regiment, Colonel Plumer's intelligence officer, arrived through the Boer lines. I met him as he was going to change.

He said, "How do you do? I am —— to be in."

I said, "How are you? I am very glad to see you, but I should be —— glad to be out."

However, there is no satisfying everybody. The country was infested by Boers and he had walked twenty-two miles that night accompanied by two natives. He is as a scout *facile princeps*, and thus eluded the hostile cordon successfully, though he had one anxious moment when he fell into the trench connecting Fort Ayr and the refugee *laager*, heard native voices, and was for some time under the impression it was the Boer trench. He was second in command of Colonel Plumer's scouts in 1896, and afterwards disappeared into Central Africa for two years, going from Chinde to Blantyre, to Lake Nyassa, then by Lake Bangueolo to the source of the Congo, thence due south through the Mashakalumbwe country to Victoria Falls, and through which country he was the first white man to pass, and from the falls to Bulawayo, where he arrived in December, 1898. Though his journeys then may have been long, arduous, and dangerous, they can scarcely have been more exciting than the short twenty-two miles he walked last night.

A quiet day. Flags of truce pass daily informing us of the condition of the wounded.

5th, Thursday. This morning Smitheman went to the brickfields with the colonel and was shot at a bit. We all told him that we were afraid we shouldn't be able to find him any entertainment as the Boers are very quiet just now, and he said we needn't trouble. However, as the morning wore on the enemy's sixteen-pounder commenced bombarding us from Game Tree and Jackal Tree and kept on the whole morning, apparently directed by a deserter, Private Hay, Protectorate Regiment, who selected his late fort and the headquarters of the Protectorate Regiment, as his main target. I shouldn't care to be Private Hay after the war as there is £50 on his head, dead or alive, and the Boers are hard up. The afternoon was pretty quiet, and the Boers have now retired all round to extreme musketry range of all the town. They livened up in the evening though, and fired a good deal, landing many bullets in the square.

6th, Friday. The morning began very quietly, and we were afraid that Smitheman would not get his introduction to "Creaky." However, in the afternoon she began, and he had a full opportunity of learning the meaning of the various sounds of the bell, the joys of the rush to the "dugout," and the philosophy with which you can see your friends in the distance shelled, when she diverted a certain portion of her fire on Cannon Kopje.

Major Goold-Adams had just shifted into a new office after his former one had been destroyed, and somewhat prematurely, for "Creaky" promptly blew it up with the first shell; fortunately it was empty at the time. They gave us a good doing and stopped for the night.

7th, Saturday. We were awakened by the big gun, which kept on all day. Smitheman was again lucky. He went up to lunch at the kopje, and then they began shelling that, so he had had most of the pleasures of Mafeking compressed into three days. They pall, however, after six months. He seemed to think we were having a harder time than he anticipated, and it is very interesting to have an outside opinion, because we are so thoroughly used to it that we do not know whether it is a bad time or not, being only convinced of two things—that the place can't fall, and that we will not get hit by a big shell if we can help it. Smitheman returned to Plumer tonight.

8th, Sunday. A quiet day. A body of women, who, at Smitheman's instigation, was endeavouring to escape towards Kanya, where food is ready for them, was turned back by the Boers. To the south a similar body was also stopped, and by direction of the Boer in charge each one was stripped, *shambokked*, and driven back naked to Mafeking. Yesterday there was a desperate fight between a party of our *Fingoes* engaged in cattle raiding and the Boers; the former were cut off and surrounded in a "pan," where they took what cover they could and defended their lives to the last. Out of a party of some thirty odd, ten or eleven got away when they repulsed the first attack of the Boers.

The Boers returned, however, with one hundred more men, and killed all but one man. They had two Maxims and a one-pound Maxim-Nordenfelt. The fight lasted twenty-five hours, and by the account of the wounded survivor, corroborated by the women who returned today, the Boers must have suffered severe loss. The survivor escaped by hiding in the reeds, and is now in hospital with a wound in his stomach. The natives were vastly outnumbered, and made a stubborn resistance with their obsolete arms against all the Boers could bring against them. Unfortunate it is that so few of many brave men escaped.

Snyman is becoming remarkably civil in his intercourse, and had sent in a letter saying he was astonished that natives had been employed cattle raiding, as they were such barbarians. They were right gallant barbarians, anyhow. Smitheman has a wonderful insight into native character, and a marvellous grasp of the Baralong. It is curious to note how the Englishman associated with the natives identifies himself with his tribe and becomes a Zulu, Baralong, *Fingoe* or Basuto with a firm belief that all other natives except his own particular tribe are no good at all and that their methods of fighting are useless. Having heard the point discussed by many of my friends and having witnessed their implicit confidence in their own particular tribe and distrust of the others, one can understand that the foreigner may see something to laugh at in an Englishman's absolute and justified confidence in the English. They call it insularity in Europe. I wonder what they would call its offspring here.

9th, Monday. Runners from the north arrived with the intelligence that Smitheman had passed them well clear of the Boer line, so we hope he is safe. The big gun has been shelling all the morning, and some of her smaller brethren have taken it up this afternoon. Many conflicting rumours, but a force of many men and guns went south on Friday night. We hope this portends the approach of our expected relief. It would be hard lines indeed, after all this dull work, not to finish the campaign in the Transvaal. The natives say the Boers are going to give us another severe doing tomorrow. The flags of truce exchange much chaff. The Boers say, "Why don't you come out and fight in the open?" and the answer is, "Come and drive us out."

The other day the Boers said to our orderly that it was very brutal sending men who had never been to sea to St. Helena, besides what would they do there? Whether he expected us to find picnic parties for them or not I do not know. I wish I were at St. Helena, one would have a chance of getting somewhere else from there. The orderly said there was plenty to do, but the Boer objected there were no horses for them to ride, and when the orderly said, "Let them ride the turtles,"

PEACEFUL TALK BETWEEN BOERS AND BRITISH.

he was very wroth.

Again, yesterday, the Boer volunteered that they, the Dutch, were knocking us about in the Free State. The orderly said, "The Free State, where is the Free State?" and the Boer said, "North of the Orange River." On the orderly's answering, "Ah! You mean New England," the Boer seemed hurt, but they are pretty civil all the same and both sides continually ask after their various friends and get answers.

10th, Tuesday. A fairly quiet day. The high velocity guns shelled our outlying posts on the western border, with occasional shots at the camp, while the big gun and the smaller ones shelled the town. Natives from the south report that the country is at present unsafe for despatch riders as, though there is no commando, there are a considerable number of Boers roaming about the country between here and Vryburg seeking whom and what they may devour and under no immediate control.[2]

11th, Wednesday. We were awakened this morning by the big gun and had a very heavy day's shelling. I went out for a ride and up to Fort Ayr. They were shelling from every side in all directions and kept it up till nearly noon, Mr. Greenfield is at present doing his month's detachment duty at Fort Ayr. It is not an enlivening spot, being built underground, and as you are continually sniped it is impossible to emerge therefrom except at night or by means of a long rear trench leading to the refugees' *laager*. It is garrisoned by thirty men, a Maxim and a seven-pounder. On the western front the Boers made an attack on two of our outlying posts. They advanced to within four hundred and fifty yards, but after losing some ten or a dozen men they retired.

During the day they planted some thirty shells into the women's *laager*. To all their heavy bombardment we answered not a shot, but in the evening when they were dismantling the big gun the Hotchkiss opened on her with good effect, apparently wounding or killing several of the crowd round her. She immediately opened fire on the town and struck the Dutch church with great violence. After she had ceased firing the Hotchkiss opened again and failed to get a further reply. Score:—Hotchkiss four, big gun three.

12th, Thursday. This morning the big gun has disappeared and is supposed to be in McMullin's *laager*. She has not fired, and with the exception of the five-pounder we have had a quiet day.

---

2. Later they themselves were devoured.

Several wagons with escorts have *trekked* from the *laager* and they are apparently busily engaged in packing up others.

A pigeon left Colonel Plumer yesterday at noon arriving here in forty minutes, and runners in this morning brought Her Majesty's message to Colonel Baden-Powell and news of Lieutenant Smitheman's safe arrival at Colonel Plumer's camp.

Captain McLaren is, I am glad to say, better, and in the hands of a skilful German surgeon who thinks he will do all right.

The rains have begun again which is fortunate for us. Had it not been for the exceptionally rainy season I do not know what the cattle would have done or how we could have held out.

13th, Friday. A quiet day. We were only shelled today with the five-pounder and the one-pound Maxim and so we are quite quiet. Colonel Baden-Powell has had an erection built on the top of the headquarter house from whence he looks out and can control the Mafeking defences like the captain of a ship, shouting his instructions down a speaking tube to the headquarter bomb proof, which are thence telephoned on to the parties whom it may concern, so that he can personally turn on the tap of any portion of the defences he may think fit.

14th, Saturday. This morning there was quite a lively amount of shelling. One shell burst in Fort Ayr and killed two of its garrison. Personally I started for a ride, but finding it rather livelier than I cared for made it a pretty short one. One must get exercise, but there is no particular object in getting shot unnecessarily. Last night Colonel Plumer's column endeavoured to send us in some hundred head of cattle which we want. It was a moonlight night and the Boers must have been informed of their advent for they waylaid them very effectually, killing and wounding many, as well as their native drivers, and capturing the rest. This is a bore, but, however, we can get on without them and we shall get them back shortly. In consequence of this diversion they were firing pretty well all night. Easter Day tomorrow. We can do very well without the Easter eggs the Boers send us, and as our hens have ceased to lay we shall get none of our own. Our hot cross buns were represented by a cross being stamped on our scanty bread ration. I rather hope that this is the last feast of any sort that the garrison of Mafeking will celebrate under siege conditions.

Colonel Vyvyan was very lucky in securing a beautiful specimen of a sixteen-pounder, Vicker's Maxim, which passed over his head and

A SHELL BURSTING IN THE NATIVE QUARTER.

did not explode. In the scurry for the shell he secured it, as he was mounted. They are using a new sort of one-pound Maxim and not being quite able to reach the women's *laager* with it they planted six shells in the hospital. Yesterday one of Colonel Plumer's wounded died while undergoing an operation in the Boer camp and they sent his body in last night.

I cannot understand the Boer, and have given it up as a bad job. He appears to have no laws and few instincts, and to be totally irresponsible. Sometimes he behaves exceedingly well, and at other times remarkably ill, and you can never calculate what his conduct will be under any given circumstances. General Snyman is sanctimonious and a hypocrite, and seems to look upon truth as an unnecessary portion of his field outfit. Commandant Botha is a good sportsman, and well liked on their side of the border, and is a kindly dispositioned man. Snyman is a strict disciplinarian as Boers go, whilst Botha seems an easier going man. If Snyman has been away, on his return the more or less quiet existence we have led, thanks to Botha, is immediately disturbed, and heavy shell fire commences.

Snyman is not popular in Mafeking, the inhabitants of which look upon him as a combination of liar, fanatic and woman killer, and, generally speaking, an infernal nuisance. The Dutch say he is very venturesome; he will, I believe, venture a lot to obtain cattle, but apparently less to obtain Mafeking. The Boers at the outset could have captured Mafeking for about half the lives they have expended in their various futile attacks. They can never capture it now, and the one ardent desire of the garrison is that they may only endeavour to do so.

15th, Sunday, Easter-day. A quiet day and the big gun still undiscoverable. The various churches were well attended at all the services. In the afternoon we had sports, organized by Captain Cowan and the officers of the Bechuanaland Rifles. They were a great success, and the costume race, won by Mr. Daniel, B.S.A.P., dressed as a hospital nurse, Mr. Dunlop Smith, A.VD., as the "*Geisha*" second, Captain Scholefield, B.S.A.P., as a bride third, was a great success, and one of the most amusing contests we have had here.

Yesterday it was indeed bad luck for the poor fellows of Fort Ayr garrison who had remained under cover during shell fire and thought it was all over, for when Troopers Molloy and Hassell came out to get their coffee the last high velocity sixteen-pound shell struck the sand bags overhead, killing Molloy dead and mortally wounding Hassell, breaking both his legs. Mr. Greenfield tells me the way he bore his sufferings was literally heroical, complaining not at all, and only asking for a cigarette.

I have not previously alluded to the "sowen" porridge, which is now a part of the rations, and has for a long time done much to solve the question of the food supply of Mafeking. It was first made by Private Sims out of the husks of oats for the consumption of himself and sundry of his comrades, but on this fact being ascertained by the indefatigable Captain Ryan, Sims was put on to make it on a larger scale for the natives. The European portion of the garrison and inhabitants gladly bought it, and it is now, as I said before, an acceptable portion of the daily rations. The natives, too, have had great windfalls lately in the matter of locusts, which are really not bad eating, and at any rate much appreciated by them.

The feeding of the natives, indeed, at all times a difficult question, is, I may say, practically solved, except in the case of the Shangans. These unfortunate devils, who are equally repulsive, morally and physically, as far as I have seen, are detested by the other natives, and consequently it is very hard to look after them properly. The Basutos, Zulus, &c., come to be fed naturally, whereas the Shangan is like a wild beast, and only seems to crawl away and die. So much is this so that on Mr. Vere Stent's ordering his Basuto servant to make some soup for a starving Shangan he had picked up, the Basuto indignantly protested that "the Shangans were bad men and killed missionaries," however, the man in question was rescued in time and is still living. They form luckily an insignificant proportion of the native community.

After the siege is over and the queen has got her own again it is to be hoped that the unswerving loyalty of the Baralongs will not be overlooked. You hear on all sides that the Baralongs are not a fighting race, and the Zulus and any other race you may mention would wipe them out. Incidentally the Zulus tried to in their big trek north, and the wily Baralong, fighting his usual fight, had considerably the best of it.

In more modern times he successfully withstood the Boers, not, however, an attack on the present scale. After the first day's shelling the mouthpiece of the Baralong tribe, Silas Molemo, came up to Mr. Bell, Resident Magistrate, and said to him, "Never mind this we will stick to you and see it through," which they certainly have done. They are not a tribe who would make a dashing attack or to use the expression "be bossed up" to do things they don't particularly want to, but given a defensive position they will hang on to it for all they are worth as they have proved many times during the war in their defence of their *stadt*. They have had their cattle raided, their out-lying homesteads destroyed, their crops for this year are *nil*, and all through a time when the outlook to a native mind must have seemed most black they have unswervingly and uncomplainingly stuck to us and never hesitated to do anything they were called upon to do.

I cannot do better than give an account of the unsuccessful attempt to bring in cattle from Colonel Plumer. Mathakong, the leader of the party, had forty men under his command. He and the Baralongs have so far been very successful in getting in cattle; by profession a cattle thief, but only on a large scale, there is nothing mean about Mathakong. Colonel Plumer selected some hundred head of cattle in good condition and it was these that the party endeavoured to bring in. When they were some distance out it was reported to Mathakong that the Boers knew that they were coming and were going to try to intercept them. However, as he had been given to understand that it was desirable to get the cattle in he determined to make the attempt, as at any rate they might get some in, and if he stayed where he was the Boers would probably surround him. The Boers got on both flanks of the cattle, assisted by the Rapulanas (the Rietfontein rebel natives), and heavy firing began.

The Baralongs pushed forward with cattle falling all round them and behind the bodies of the cattle kept up a running fight until all their ammunition was gone. They stuck to them till only fifteen head were left, and then when they left, the Boers came up cheering loudly. There were two wounded men amongst the cattle and the Boers according to their custom came up and interrogated them and then shot one and cut the other's throat. The Baralongs then came into Mafeking dragging old Mathakong with them as they could not otherwise persuade him to leave the live cattle. He was much upset by the loss of the cattle, but the fight did not worry him at all, and he said that had the cattle not been in such good condition he would have rushed them along faster and got most of them in. This, however, is only one of the many cases in which the Baralongs have done, or have endeavoured to do good service. They lost four killed and seven wounded and account for their small loss by the protection afforded them by the herd amongst which they fought their running fight.

16th, Monday. Fairly quiet day. The Boers shelled the western outpost and brickfields. I went down to the brickfields to see Captain Brown, Cape Police, who is in charge and was in charge when he occupied the Boer advanced trench. Since then he has been wounded, but is now back at duty again. He told me that the idea of the Boers was apparently that we should not enter the trench until the morning after they had vacated it, but our doing so the night before and cutting the wire had frustrated their amiable intention of blowing up our men and presumably rushing the brickfields in the confusion. The other day, a Cape policeman met a Transvaal policeman with a white flag (between these forces in times of peace a very good feeling prevails) and chaffed him, saying, "Why don't you blow your mine up."

"Ah!" said the latter, "you were too slim for us there."

Houndsditch, the old Boer trench, has now been converted into a strong fortification for ourselves, and the brickfields generally are a far more desirable place for residence, the several Boer trenches now being nine hundred to one thousand two hundred yards away. They have some very good marksmen in their trenches however, and make things very warm for our advanced trenches. A Cape Boy exposed himself for a moment two or three days ago and was picked off through the head by a Martini at once, and in the very few open spaces which of course they have got accurately ranged they shoot remarkably close. The brickfields are now garrisoned by the Cape Police and Cape Boys under Captain Brown and Lieutenants Murray and Currie.

The big gun is still conspicuous by its absence, and it is reported to have gone to Pretoria. If that be so it is the greatest sign so far that the Boers feel hopeless about taking the town and the point may be fairly scored off against any point they may have scored against us yet.

There was a wedding this morning between a private of the Bechuanaland Rifles and a Dutch girl, he cannot talk Dutch nor she English. Let us hope that it is a good omen of the future settlement of South Africa with the British as "Boss."

This morning, too, three ambulances were seen coming in from the North, and an ambulance and five waggons went in that direction, so Plumer may have had a successful "scrap," at any rate, we all hope so.

These high velocity guns seem beautiful weapons, I must confess that in common with the rest of the garrison I should dearly like to see them tried on the Boer. It is all very well to be an expert in artillery, but ours is not the most agreeable way of gaining the experience.

17th, Tuesday. The question of firewood and indeed all fuel has of late been a somewhat serious one to Mafeking, and as the cold season is coming on or rather is beginning, increases in importance daily, consequently Mafeking has had to sacrifice its scanty supply of trees. Probably the residents in their vicinity wish, if they had to be cut down, it had been done at the commencement of the siege, for it seems as if the Boer artillery when having no mark in particular but the town in general had mainly aimed at the trees, at any rate, when they were merely idly shelling the majority of shells fell in their neighbourhood. It will, I fear, put the general appearance of the town back for some years.

With the exception of perfunctory shelling in the brickfields, we have had a quiet day and the big gun is still absent. Indeed, now so far have our outlying trenches been pushed that except from the big gun and quick-firers, we experience but little annoyance in the town itself. During the last week our runners have been most successfully stopped, but before this we have been fortunate enough to get London papers three months old, and the Court House has been turned into a reading-room, where the papers are daily eagerly devoured by all conditions of men and women too. Everybody at home seems very pleased with Mafeking, and we here feel really proud of the way our fellows are fighting in the South and the way everybody is turning up to fight. It should be a fine object-lesson to the Continentals. In many ways they must have had a more amusing time than we have had and fighting on a much larger scale, for this sort of fighting after the first two months is about the dullest sort of entertainment you can well imagine: they so hopelessly overwhelm us in artillery that we cannot get out to have a go at them.

Indeed, any sortie must resolve itself into storming one of their forts which we are not strong enough to do, and so the forts on either side face each other, fire at each other, but otherwise leave each other severely alone; and outside their zone of fire their artillery takes up whatever position it thinks fit and shells whatever portion of defences or town it feels inclined to. One advantage in a long dragging performance like this is that neither side seems in any particular hurry and a very wet day generally means a certain immunity from fire. Yesterday we had a heavy thunderstorm, and the first flash of lightening exploded one of our mines in front of the brickfields simultaneously with the thunderclap. I felt the ground shake and thought it was a particularly heavy clap of thunder.

The mine which was charged with ten pounds of captured nitro-glycerine blew a tremendous hole in the ground, and was, generally speaking, a great success, so what would have happened had their carefully prepared two hundred and fifty pound mine gone off, or what would have been left of Mafeking, I do not like to think. The mine is now recharged and repaired, but I am afraid the Boers have a nasty suspicious disposition which will prevent them from sampling it.

The Cadet Corps have been lately doing their messages mounted on donkeys captured from the Boers. Like the other mounted corps, however, their ranks are gradually being depleted for the soup kitchen. This corps is formed of all the boys of Mafeking, ranging from nine years upwards. It does all the foot orderly work, thereby sparing several more men for the trenches, and is dressed in khaki with "smasher" hats and a yellow *puggarree*. It is commanded by a youth, Sergeant-Major Goodyear, the son of Captain Goodyear, who was wounded in the brickfields, and is directly supervised by Lord Edward Cecil. It drills regularly, and the boys are wonderfully smart.

Our acetylene search lights on the principle of the duplex heliograph repeat the signals from a central station to the stations all round the outposts, and answer very well. These and all the signalling arrangements are under the charge of Sergeant-Major Moffatt, late Carbineers, who has been very successful on several occasions in tapping the Boers' helio messages. He has also invented a new acetylene signalling lamp, which he has patented, and which he claims can be worked (instead of the helio) on a cloudy day as well as at night. From what I have seen of the lamp I think his claims are well founded.

18th, Wednesday. Desultory shelling. Last night eleven native women tried to get out, nine were killed and two were wounded. This, in spite of repeated protests of Colonel Baden-Powell, who has pointed out that Snyman continually shells the native village, and that when the women try to escape they are flogged by day and shot by night. Botha, on hearing of the occurrence, expressed his great regret and promised to look after the wounded. Last night, too, the Boers were blowing up the line to the south, about five miles out.

19th, Thursday. The Boers are continually blowing up the line southward, and great activity prevails around all the laagers, more particularly at McMullins's. Straws show which way the wind blows, and we hope this renewed liveliness portends the approach of relief. A quiet day. The recent heavy rains have caused a lot of fever here, but in spite of that the health of the garrison is on the whole good.

20th, Friday. Runners arrived with papers and a letter giving an account of the murder of young Dennison at Vryburg. He, it appears, was wounded, and the Boers shot him in cold blood. In the same papers we read accounts of the excellent treatment received by Cronje and the other Boer prisoners, and the infamous treatment accorded to Colonial prisoners of war by the Boers. Having contravened every known law of war, except perhaps poisoning wells, it would seem only reasonable that they should be treated judicially, as they claim to be a civilized race, and given a chance of explaining their breaches of the Geneva Convention. Failing to do this they should be accorded the justice for which they are always clamouring.

It appears to me less important to conciliate the rebel Dutch than to avoid stirring up the indignation which is expressing itself very freely amongst the loyal Colonials at the ridiculously lenient way in which the rebels are treated, and as the Bond Attorney-General cannot see his way to proceed against them, it would surely be possible to replace him by an official who was not an avowed sympathiser of theirs. The rebels, so far, apparently have had really a very good time of it. They have looted their loyal neighbours' property, and harried their cattle and farms, murdering them, when so inclined, to their hearts' content, and now are apparently neither going to be asked to pay for their amusement or even disgorge their plunder. You do not as a rule expect the conquered to be satisfied with the victor's settlement of a war, but apparently in our case we are going to pacify our enemies at the expense of our friends. However, I suppose the matter will square itself, and the Colonial troops will not trouble to take prisoners to undergo a farce of a trial.

21st, Saturday. Lord Roberts's message was received yesterday, stating that owing to unforeseen delays the relief column would not be able to reach us by May 18th as originally promised, and asking us to husband our provisions beyond that date. The news had no depressing effect on the town or garrison, and everybody is resolved to undergo anything sooner than surrender. As regards the healthy portion of the garrison the task is a fairly easy one, but for the sick (which are daily increasing in number), the women and children, and the native population to subsist on gradually decreasing rations is indeed hard. Luxuries are, of course, a thing of the past, and it is only with the utmost economy of the necessities of life that our supplies will be equal to the task.

However, by the time you get this, the matter will be settled one way or another, but as long as the Union Jack is still flying, any privations will be cheerfully welcomed. The rations now are a quarter-pound of bread, half-pound of meat, supplemented with horseflesh and "*sowen*" porridge. It is due to the care of the authorities, and mostly so to Captain Ryan, A.S.C., whose skilful, painstaking, and unwearied manipulation of supplies in the way of calculation, storage, development, and their issue, that we are able even now to live in comparative comfort.

He has organised his butcheries and bakeries most admirably. I went round the stores the other day, and paid a visit to his sieving-room, where he has constructed large sieves to sift the fine oatmeal for bread purposes from the husks which are used for making "*sowen*" porridge, (one hundred pounds of oats producing twenty pounds of fine meal). There I found a dozen or so coal-black individuals under the superintendence of an Englishman, sifting whilst grinning through their covering of flour, and constituting an interesting and very comical spectacle. There is nothing wasted. We eat the fine meal and the "*sowen*" porridge, the horses eat the refuse from the "*sowen*" porridge, while we again eat the horses. As a local poet remarks—

Till the Queen shall have her own again, for the flag we have always flown,
If we cannot live on the fat of the land, we'll fight on the horse and 'sowen.'

Today Mrs. Winter and her little boy, aged six, walked to the edge of the town, where recently it has been quiet, but the sight of a petticoat in fancied security was too much for the Boers, for they immediately sniped at her, fortunately, however, without effect.

They were shelling the brickfields today, but were otherwise quiet. They, however, nearly hit Colonel Baden-Powell with a shell when he was in that quarter.

22nd, Sunday. A quiet day. The concert in the afternoon was a great success, and Colonel Baden-Powell as usual "brought down the house" in his musical sketches. On reading some old papers I see the Boers have the consummate impudence to protest against our conduct of the war. Now I wish clearly to point out that I do not try to saddle the whole Boer nation with the conduct of some of their worst characters, but the lower class Boer is, in many cases, no better than a savage and sometimes, in the case of educated Kaffirs, considerably worse. I am not trying to pile up atrocities against them, but *à propos* of the subject generally, the following facts are somewhat interesting. George Umfazwi, the head *Fingoe*, a Christian, is a leading member of the Rev. W. H. Weekes's congregation in the native location.

One night he went out cattle-raiding, in charge of a mixed party of *Fingoes* and Baralongs. These parties, as I have said before, go out on their own initiative, and sell their plunder to the government. Soon after starting they came upon the body of a Baralong woman, who, when endeavouring to escape, had had her throat cut. Naturally the Baralongs were more than annoyed, and vowed to kill all the Dutch women they might come across. Umfazwi, however, told them that if they persisted in their intentions he and the *Fingoes* would have nothing more to do with them.

In the course of their raid they occupied a Dutch homestead, from which they were fired upon by Dutchmen. In the house were three Dutch women, whom the natives did not touch, only taking the cattle and returning to Mafeking. In the next raid, Umfazwi and his *Fingoes* were surrounded, as I told you in a former account, and, after a hard fight, were all killed—no quarter being given. I was talking yesterday to Major Anderson, E.A.M.C., and he said, in the course of the conversation, that he preferred a savage warfare, for then you knew what to expect, and that if he had to go out again, he would sooner not take a Red Cross flag, as on each occasion on which he had done so, it had drawn the fire; whereas, when he went out without, he only took his chance with the rest.

23rd, Monday. Today they shelled the town, doing no damage. They employed a new sort of nine-pounder shell, which will make a nice lamp stand. Two deaths from fever last night, and I fear there will be another death today. These late rains have brought out a sort of typhoid malaria.

A most interesting account, from a private soldier's point of view, has been contributed by Private G. Hyslop, Bechuanaland Rifles, to *The Glasgow Weekly Herald*, and though his sources of accurate information are naturally somewhat limited, it is a most fair and intelligent account of the siege.

24th, Tuesday. We received glorious news last night, but it seems almost too good to be true, namely, that Lord Roberts had surrounded the Boers at Kronstadt, and had given them twenty-four hours to surrender, and that Lord Methuen had reached Klerksdorp. It is quite possible, but still one does not like to believe it before it is verified, and it is after all a rumour. On the face of it, it seems probable, and that it is a continuation of his turning movement. If so, the Boers in these parts are nicely out-manoeuvred, and we look for our Relief Column following Methuen's tract as far as Border Siding, and then coming up the line.

Automatic relief, so glibly talked about in some papers, will not be of much use to us, for what we most require is provisions. I saw it stated in an article in *The Times* that Kimberley and ourselves were of no strategical importance in the campaign, but I totally disagree with this idea. Had Mafeking and Kimberley fallen at first, or had Cronje been able to disregard these two isolated places and swept down south, the Colony, to a great extent, would have fallen into his hands. The troops in the South would have had a far greater extent of country to reconquer, and Mafeking at any rate must have eventually fallen. The natives would have lost confidence, the Boers would have retained possession of the line and the rolling stock from the Vaal River to the north, Rhodesia would have been open to attack, and the whole conditions of the war entirely changed, and not changed in our favour.

I suppose this also holds good of Ladysmith, but there, of course, the Boers would have left a considerable force in their rear. I think it was the half-heartedness of the Boers in only partially invading the Colony and Natal and remaining to nibble at the tempting baits of apparently two unprotected towns, which gave the troops coming out an advantage which they never would have had had the Boers made one dash for Capetown. And even now, though in a very much less degree, I consider this town of strategical importance. We keep a large number of Boers in our proximity, and the Boers in the neighbouring districts are more concerned about preventing our relief than in opposing the force from which the really imminent danger threatens.

And if it be true that Lord Methuen is at Klerksdorp, the Boers in these parts will have no earthly weight in the decisive portion of the campaign. Why they should wish to take Mafeking except to score one trick, as all other advantages they have gained they have since lost, it is hard to say. Their chance of invading Rhodesia is gone, the crossings of the Vaal River are in our hands. There are no stores now in Mafeking and beyond the bare temporary possession, they would gain nothing at all, added to which I should have thought that by this time they might have learnt that they were not going to have even a temporary possession.

The verdict of the court martial which tried Lieutenant Murchison for the murder of Mr. Parslow and sentenced him to death, has come back confirmed by Lord Roberts, who, however, has commuted the sentence to one of penal servitude for life. Murchison was at one time a major in the Royal Artillery, and so far as I know him personally, I do not consider him responsible for his actions.

The Rhodesian postal authorities notified us today that press telegrams (owing to the congestion of the lines) would be taken off the wires at Umtali, sent by train to Beira, and then be re-telegraphed to London *via* Lorenzo Marques. The press has naturally protested strongly, as their course of action will probably entail a delay of a week. The postal arrangements throughout the campaign have been most infamous; whether the fault lies at Cape Town or Bulawayo I know not, but in any case some abominably careless official should be hauled over the coals. We have consistently got letters out from here which have been received at home, and it simply means total imbecility or inexcusable idleness on the part of responsible authorities if we are unable to receive letters in the same way.

Most people here naturally say it is the fault of the Bond Government, and though they have deserved hanging many times over, I do not think this particular crime can be laid at their door, though the absence of our guns certainly may. Mr. Schreiner has, I see, protested against the Boers being sent to St. Helena. I am unaware if he has protested against our being detained here. He also states that people misjudge him and he seems annoyed. He has only been judged by his actions, which here, as well as elsewhere, are deplored. However, this savours of politics, and is therefore somewhat out of my province.

*25th, Wednes*day. Last night we received warning from native sources that the Boers intended to make an attack on the town today, and that it was to be a personally conducted tour by young Eloff, who had been sent from Pretoria to take Mafeking or die in the attempt. He is, or ought to be, very much alive, for his operations were conducted from a safe distance and the town is much as usual. Of late we have been so dull here, that a considerable amount of fictitious enthusiasm was boiled up over this impending attack. Mr. Hamilton of *The Times* thought it was good enough to sleep in the advanced trench, but the more wary and possibly less enthusiastic, amongst which I include myself, considered a good bed was preferable to an indifferent one.

TOPOGRAPHICAL SKETCH OF MAFEKING.

However, I looked out cartridges and laid out weapons when I went to bed, but didn't wake any earlier next morning, and was roused by Ronny Moncreiffe shouting out, "Get up, there is a battle going on." I vainly tried to persuade him to allow me to remain in bed until the enemy were near enough to be dangerous, but he insisted that I should get up and look on. I decided there was no immediate necessity for weapons, and rode off to the nearest telescope to find the enemy. At the B.S.A.P. fort I found the officers of the Protectorate Regiment just coming off the roof, yawning and looking very bored. They told me what had happened up till my arrival, and I went and looked through the telescope for a bit at our friends the enemy whom we could clearly see. They were firing their guns and maintaining a heavy musketry fire, though in somewhat purposeless manner about one thousand five hundred yards from our advanced trench.

A gentleman on horseback, presumably the dashing Eloff, galloped out from the western *laager*, and with many gesticulations and fruitless haranguing endeavoured to get them to advance, but they were obdurate. They pitched one or two shells up by the fort, which were promptly annexed by *piccaninnies*, as the majority did not burst, and they killed a nigger, and a ricochet hit old Whitfield in the stomach, but, owing to the width of his figure, the bullet did not penetrate. I think what put them off most was our absolute silence. We did not fire at all except some twenty rounds at some Boers that had been ambushed in the culvert, which had the effect of driving them into some bushes, where they hid for a couple of hours.

I really think the people surrounding us here have honestly had enough of it, and it will take a better man than young Eloff to bring them up to the scratch, though there are certainly more Boers about here than there have been for some time. The object of this particular attack was to draw our fire and make us disclose our positions on the western front, and the result was a most conspicuous failure. We refused to be drawn by the feint, and so the real attack, which was supposed to be concealed elsewhere, was never able to develop. Apparently the plan was good, like General Trochu's, but it has at any rate so tired them that they have been unable to do anything since.

26th, Thursday. Received my first letters since this abominable isolation commenced. One from Weston-Jarvis and another from Smitheman. Weston is very cheerful. Smitheman, extravagant as regards paper, and rather sparing of words and ink; I also received some *Morn-*

ing Posts, and see that I have successfully established communication, which is satisfactory.

27th, Friday. More runners, but thanks to the usual breakdown of the Beira-Salisbury line, dates and news are so mixed, and the contending forces seem so extraordinarily and intricately involved with each other, that we have given up trying to understand how things really are going. It doesn't very much matter, as the result is a foregone conclusion, and at the worst can only be shortly delayed. One thing is amusing, and that is to see the various reasons different countries give for not offering to mediate.

28th, Saturday. Nothing doing. Preparing for the tournament to-morrow. My *kaffir* wishes to go and join Plumer. He doesn't approve of the food supply of Mafeking. I thought I should never get rid of him. Thank goodness the brute has gone now. He has been a sort of "old man of the sea" to me. I only kept him because he appeared generally in small health, but when he flung his rations into the middle of the square yesterday, I thought it was high time for him to be off. The last few days the enemy has been more busy on the north-eastern front, and established themselves in a sniping trench seven hundred yards from our advanced trench, and made themselves rather a nuisance. We, however, made it so warm for them that they are concluded to have withdrawn, but everywhere else, since the 25th, they have been fairly quiet.

29th, Sunday. A most successful tournament, and almost up to Agricultural Hall form. Most regiments in the service represented, and the sword mounted and bayonet dismounted both particularly good. It was trying work judging on half rations, but well worth it to see such good sport.

What a funny little Frenchman that Prince Henri d'Orleans must be? His compliments to a French comic paper on caricatures of the English would almost entitle him to a prominent position on its staff, where, at any rate, he would score a greater success than posing as an unemployed patriot. By the bye, was he not once attached to the British Army, and if so, whence this venom? But of tea-table tacticians and sofa strategists you must, indeed, have more than enough. Reading the papers from home one sees excellent persons with presumably nothing to do, recommending people generally to turn the other cheek to the smiter; personally, I and, indeed, most of my neighbours, think that the smiter has had quite sufficient chances at our entire carcasses during the last few months, and if they feel themselves so imbued with an overflowing Christian spirit, I should suggest their taking a turn themselves.

I do not love the Boer, and I don't think I shall until the Boer loves me. There is only one way to obtain his respect and even toleration, and that is by proving yourself the better man. There will then be peace in the country which, at the present moment, there is not. I do think, too, that people at home should not be so free in their comments upon intelligence from this part of the world. For many years I have read Mr. Baillie Grohmann's letters on big game shooting with much interest. I have also tried to shoot big game and Boers with about equally moderate success. I do assert most emphatically that the Boers use explosive bullets. I have seen the bullets, heard the bullets, and picked up the base of bullets with fulminate caps in them. They were not Mauser bullets, they were not expanding bullets, they were explosive bullets pure and simple, and the Boers have confessed to their use.

Therefore, I think it would only have been fair had Mr. Baillie Grohmann waited to know on what grounds people out here have made these assertions, before writing a somewhat conclusive letter in which the main point appeared to be that there was no such thing as an explosive Mauser bullet. It is rather hard on some hundreds of thousands of Englishmen who happen to be serving their country out here, that because they are on that service they should be immediately considered to be destitute of that sense of fair play with which the race generally is credited, and I am sure that Mr. Baillie Grohmann himself, would be the first to admit it. We don't expect much more from a Boer than a bullet, and as far as we know have not particularly grumbled at their using explosive ones, but it is hard lines to be told they didn't when we mention the fact. I personally felt a sense of great disappointment that I was not reading Mr. Baillie Grohmann's usual letters to *The Field*, instead of this one in *The Morning Post*.

We are threatened with another attack tomorrow. I hope it will be more productive of bloodshed than the last, because we can then clear them off a bit, and I hate feeling hungry, as do most of us.

Colonel Baden-Powell has just received a missive from young Eloff, in which he states that he sees in a *Bulawayo Chronicle* that we have concerts, balls, tournaments, and cricket matches on Sundays, and it will be very agreeable to his men to come in and participate as they find it dull outside. Colonel Baden-Powell has answered that he thinks perhaps the return match should be postponed until we have finished the present one and that as we are now two hundred not out, and Snyman, Cronje, &c., have not been successful he would suggest a further change of bowling. With such mild japes we pass the time away, but we shot a Dutchman this morning all the same.

A bad joke in these times is worth more than a good pint of porridge, as the former will go round whereas the latter will certainly not. It is very edifying work trying to get fat on laughter and sleep, but hunger is not a very amusing form of entertainment. They have recently manufactured brawn of horse hide. It doesn't sound very appetising but the stock disappeared with marvellous rapidity. One cannot help thinking that after all even though we be hungry out here, yet we have the glamour of war over us, whereas at home in the Metropolis one knows hundreds of men are worse off than ourselves. It is to be hoped that our impotent sympathisers will feed the people they can reach, who, after all, want it just as much as we do.

30th, Monday. Very tired and stiff after the tournament. I feel as if all the competitors had been beating me with big sticks. Talking of sticks and Doctor Leyds, which always seem associated in my mind, I bought half a dozen very nice ones yesterday, I hope Dr. Leyds is having a good time now. I fancy he will have a moderate one when the war is over, as most people directly blame him for any discomforts they may have undergone. It is only natural for a Dutchman to fight, but for the man who pulls the strings and risks other people's skins with the utmost heroism seven thousand miles off, you do not feel a great amount of affection or respect, more particularly when he is living on the fat of the land and you are rather hungry. Besides, the fellow is an infernal thief; he has battened on these unfortunate peasants for many years, and at the first pinch of fighting flies and leaves them. I have no use for a creature like that.

I was rather amused to hear Sergeant Cooke, of the Bechuanaland Rifles, report having slain a Dutchman this morning. He wasn't in the least elated, and in a shamefaced sort of way said he was afraid it wasn't a sporting shot. He couldn't have been more upset if he had shot a hen pheasant sitting, but to anyone else the episode was distinctly amusing.

1st May, Tuesday. We expect a mail today, and this dashing fellow Eloff promised us another attack. He has made it. It was the usual sort of performance, and they blazed away for two or three hours and didn't hit anybody. I got up and looked on, because I felt I ought to, but I was rather cross and very bored. If the fools want to fight, why don't they do it? They are doing themselves no good, and not attaining any object whatsoever. Colonel Baden-Powell told them some months ago they would not take Mafeking "by sitting and looking at the place," but even now, if they would sacrifice two or three thousand men, they might get in, but I am afraid they will never try.

They make me quite angry, they are so stupid. Here they are, daily losing one or two men, and the greatest success they can show is a few stolen cows, whereas if they would come on and fight properly they wouldn't lose very many more men than they have already, and we should have a chance of a show. Seriously speaking though, it is their duty to take this place, and it is very disheartening waiting for them to try to. We got our pigeon mails today; unfortunately, no news whatsoever. We have not received any decisive news or had any optimistic rumour confirmed for weeks, and in fact our last good news is Cronje's mop up. Isn't there an old figure in some square dance or other called the *chassez croissee*? It seems to be fashionable out here. I don't like square dances or slow generals.

As I telegraphed to you this morning my general sensation is that of an aching void. The only satisfaction I can derive therefrom is the certainty that most of my friends and acquaintances will be much amused at my being kept quiet anywhere on short commons. Tom Greenfield is looking terribly hungry, but then with his length he naturally takes more filling up than ordinary mortals. Godley, too, looks as if he could do with a bit more, but he always is thin. We have got a very tall lot of men here, Cecil, Tom Greenfield, Godley, Fitzclarence, Bentinck, all make an ordinary six-foot individual feel small, and McKenna isn't exactly short. If we have length represented we also have breadth, which even our present rations are unable to reduce. I am certainly not going to quote a nominal roll of these individuals, as they are fine strong men and I can't get away.

2nd, Wednesday. This morning firing is going on. I suppose another attack. I will go out and see. One rather funny incident in connection with the Boer attack took place yesterday. As a rule they knock off for breakfast, but yesterday they kept it up till some time past 8 o'clock, so at 8 o'clock punctually the natives left their trenches with their tins to draw their porridge, absolutely disregarding the Boer fire which was renewed at intervals all day. It is perfectly incredible how we have pushed them back, for within the area where our advanced trenches now are I recollect seeing a horse-battery of theirs in action during the first few days of the siege. They take particular care not to play those games now. I only wish they would. This sort of drivel relieves one's feelings, even if one can't see relief.

3rd, Thursday. Firing yesterday and today was not of any value; they kept it up off and on all day. I sat on the roof with the officers of the Bechuanaland Rifles, and looked on till we got bored. The operation of getting on to and off the roof again was far more dangerous than the ordinary Boer battle. This evening I rode round the guards with Major Panzera. It would take a more enterprising Boer than we have run up against to get in. Major Panzera has a theory that he can't be hit; I haven't, however. Both our theories are good enough viewed from the light of experience.

The Germans participating in the defence of the town are going to be photographed. I feel sorry for the German emperor not being here. He would enjoy this war thoroughly.

I heard from Weston-Jarvis this morning. He wrote a very cheery letter. At last they appear to be making some effort to relieve us. Why on earth they didn't try before, Heaven only knows! It seems a perfectly simple operation for any man of any ordinary sense, but really it doesn't much matter in the long run whether it is a month or two sooner or later. I also see the "Baron" is coming down to relieve us. I hope he won't fall on his head and get stretched out as he usually persists in doing. We are always meeting each other in some old ship or other, or in some out of the way continent, but certainly I never expected to be relieved by the "Baron" in the middle of Africa; however, the more pals that roll up the better.

4th, Friday. Absolute quiet. My last letters have fallen into the Dutchmen's hands. They will be nice light reading for them, as they were barely complimentary. I do not expect to be popular after this war. When one is tired and bored out here, it is very refreshing to be able to abuse all and sundry, and think that one need not settle up for another two or three months.

5th, Saturday. Life is short, but temper is shorter. Runners in but no news. This morning a funeral party of the Bechuanaland Rifles marched from the hospital to the cemetery to bury the remains, I say advisedly remains, of Lance-Corporal Ironside, who, after having been wounded some two months ago, had recently had his leg amputated, and had at last died from sheer weakness. He bore his extreme suf-ferings with remarkable fortitude, pluck, and cheeriness. He was a Scotchman, from Aberdeen, and one of the best shots in the garrison. It is satisfactory to think that he had already avenged his death before he was wounded.

6th, Sunday. Today the Boers most deliberately violated the tacit Sunday truce which, at their own instigation and request, we have always observed. The whole proceedings were very peculiar. It was a fine morning, and the Sabbath calm pervading the town and the surrounding forts was manifest in the way we were all strolling about the market square. As regards myself, I had just purchased some bases of shells at Platnauer's auction mart, where the weekly auction was proceeding. The firing began, and nobody paid much attention except the officers and men belonging to the quarter at which it was appar-ently directed. They, on foot, horseback, and bicycle, dispersed head-long to their various posts. One, Mr. McKenzie, on a bicycle, striking the railway line, reached his post in four minutes and fifteen seconds, fifteen seconds too quick for the Boer he was enabled to bag.

The Boers, who on previous Sundays had displayed an inclina-tion to loot our cattle, had crept up to the dead ground east of Can-non Kopje, and hastily shot one of our cattle guard and stolen the horses and mules under his charge. It was the more annoying that they should have been successful as we were well prepared for them, and had rather anticipated this attack, having a Maxim in ambush within one hundred and fifty yards, which unfortunately jammed, and failed to polish off the lot, as it certainly ought to have done. If we had had any luck it would have been a very different story.

Directly the Maxim began the Boers nipped off their horses and running alongside of them for protection reached the cover in the fold of the ground. Unfortunately they killed poor Francis of the B.S.A.P. (the second brother who has fallen here since the fighting began) and took all the horses. It was very annoying, but a smart bit of work and I congratulate the Dutchmen, whoever they may be, who conducted it. Still it was a breach of our Sunday truce, and if all is fair in love and war the many irate spectators will have their pound of flesh to ask for later on. It really was a curious sight: lines of men impotently watch-ing the raid and behind them the shouts of the unmoved auctioneer of "Going at fifteen bob." "Last time." "Going." "Going." "Gone," and gone they were undoubtedly, but they were our horses and he was referring to some scrap iron. To cover this nefarious procedure they opened a heavy fire on various outlying forts.

We were lucky enough in the interchange of courtesies to secure a Dutchman on the railway line, and as they had practically violated the white flag our advanced posts had great shooting all the afternoon at his friends who came to try to pick him up. We buried Francis this evening. The concert was put off. A certain amount of endurance has been shown by the inhabitants and a certain amount of pluck by the defenders of the town, but prior to the Boers starting fooling (successful fooling and neatly carried out), I and several more were standing in the market square gossiping about things we did know, and things we didn't, when we happened to notice a very weak-looking child, apparently as near death as any living creature could be.

It transpired on inquiry that this infant was a Dutch one, Graaf by name. His father, a refugee, died of fever; his brother was in hospital, and he had been offered admission, which he refused, because he said that he must look after his mother. Even then, though scarcely able to cross the road, the kid was going to draw his rations. He was taken to hospital, but I think that this is about the pluckiest individual that has come under my notice, and nobody can take exception to the child, though his mother is probably one of those amiable ladies who eat our rations, betray our plans, and are always expressing a wholehearted wish for our extermination.

15th, Tuesday. News has arrived that our troops are within striking distance; "Sister Ann" performance has begun again. We are now beginning to recover from our exciting Saturday. As I wired home, it was the best day that I ever saw, and I must now try and describe it.

Just before four o'clock in the morning we were roused by heavy firing. The garrison turned out and manned the various works. We all turned up, and I went to the headquarters. Everybody got their horses ready, armed themselves as best they could, and awaited the real attack. Colonel Baden-Powell said at once the real attack would be on the *stadt*. We have had a good many attacks and don't attach much importance to them, but we did not any one of us anticipate the day's work that was in store for us. When I say anticipate, every possible preparation had been made. Well, we hung about in the cold.

After about an hour and a half the firing on the eastern front began to slacken. Trooper Waterson of the Blues, as usual, had coffee and cocoa ready at once, and we felt we could last a bit. Jokes were

BOERS FIRING THE NATIVE *STADT.*

freely bandied, and we kept saying, "When are they going to begin?" Suddenly on the west a conflagration was seen, and betting began as to how far out it was. I got on to the roof of a house, and with Mr. Arnold, of Dixon's Hotel, saw a very magnificent sight. Apparently the whole *stadt* was on fire, and with the sunrise behind us and the *stadt* in flames in front, the combination of effects was truly magnificent, if not exactly reassuring.

However, nobody seemed to mind much. Our guns, followed by the Bechuanaland Rifles, hurried across the square, men laughing and joking and saying, "we were going to have a good fight." Then came the news that the B.S.A.P. fort, garrisoned by the Protectorate Regiment, had fallen into the enemy's hands. Personally I did not believe it to be true, and started with a carbine to assure myself of the fact. I got close up to the fort, met a squadron running obliquely across its front, and though the bullets were coming from that direction could not believe but that they were our own men who were strolling about outside it. That is the worst of being educated under black powder. I saw poor Hazelrigg, who was a personal friend of mine, and whom I knew at home, shot, but did not realise who he was.

Both sides were inextricably mixed, but having ridden about, and got the hang of things, I am certain that within twenty minutes, order and confidence were absolutely restored on our side. You saw bodies of men, individuals, everybody armed with what they could get, guns of any sort, running towards the firing. A smile on every man's face, and the usual remark was, "Now we've got the beggars." The "beggars" in question were under the impression that they had got us and no doubt had a certain amount of ground for their belief. The fight then began.

At least we began to fight, for up till then no return had been made to the very heavy fusillade to which we had been subjected. I have soldiered for some years and I have never seen anything smarter or better than the way the Bechuanaland Rifles, our Artillery and the Protectorate Regiment ran down and got between the Boers and their final objective. The Boers then sent a message through the telephone to say they had got Colonel Hore and his force prisoners and that we could not touch them. Campbell, our operator, returned a few remarks of his own not perhaps wholly complimentary and the telephone was disconnected and reconnected with Major Godley.

Our main telephone wire runs through the B.S.A.P. fort. McLeod, the man in charge of the wires, commenced careering about armed with a stick and a rifle, and followed by his staff of black men with the idea of directly connecting Major Godley's fort and the headquarters. I may mention McLeod is a sailor and conducts his horse on the principle of a ship. He is perhaps the worst horseman I have ever seen and it says much for the honour of the horse flesh of Mafeking that he is still alive.

However, be that as it may, his pawky humour and absolute disregard of danger has made him one of the most amusing features of the siege. You always hear him in broad Scotch and remarkable places, but he is always where he is wanted. By this time we were settling down a bit, so were they. They looted everything they possibly could. A Frenchman got on to the roof of the fort with a bottle of Burgundy belonging to the officers' mess to drink to "*Fashoda.*" He got hit in the stomach and his pals drank the bottle.

Our men were very funny. When the Frenchmen yelled "*Fashoda,*" they said "silly beggars, their geography is wrong." I was very pleased with the whole day. I have never heard more or worse jokes made, and, no doubt, had I been umpiring, I should have put some of us out of action or at any rate given them a slight advantage. Every townsman otherwise unoccupied, who had possibly never contemplated the prospect of a fight to the finish, now turned out. Mr. Weil (and too much cannot be said for his resource through every feature of the siege) broke open his boxes, served out every species of firearms he could to every person who wanted them.

A very deaf old soldier, late of the 24th Regiment, Masters by name, asked where they were, and then proceeded to investigate in a most practical fashion. I went down to the jail which more or less commands the B.S.A.P. Fort and buildings, and had a look, and as we saw that no attack was imminent or at any rate likely to prove successful, we knocked off by parties and had our breakfast. We were beginning to kill them very nicely. Jail prisoners had all been released. Murchison, who shot Parslow, Lonie, the greatest criminal of the town, were both armed and doing their duty. We were all shooting with the greatest deliberation and effect whenever they showed themselves, and perhaps I was better pleased with being an Englishman from a sightseer's point of view than on any day since the Jubilee.

The quaint part of the whole thing was that we were shooting at our own people unwittingly. I had a cousin there, and we laughed consumedly in the evening when we exchanged notes and found that we had been shooting close to him amongst others. I don't think that

Boers' attack on a B.S.A.P. Fort

any man who was in that fight will ever think ill of his neighbour from the highest to the lowest; from our general—or, at least, he ought to be a general—to the ordinary civilian, everybody was cheerful and confident of victory. We had had a long seven months' wait, and at last we were having our decisive fight.

After breakfast (like giants refreshed) we began shooting again. I cannot tell you who did well, but I can assure you that no man did badly. Besides the men there were ladies. Mrs. Buchan and Miss Crawford worked most calmly and bravely under fire. All the other ladies did their duty too. Whilst the fight was developing, Mrs. Winter was running about getting us coffee. Her small son, aged six, was extremely wroth with me because I ordered him under shelter. Then commenced what you may call the next phase of the fight. Captain Fitzclarence and his squadron, with Mr. Swinburne and Mr. Bridges, came down through the town to join hands with Captain Marsh's squadron, and then with Lord Charles Bentinck's squadron and the Baralongs, the whole under Major Godley, were now going to commence to capture the Boers.

I must endeavour to describe the situation. Eloff's attack was clever and determined. He had seven hundred men and had advanced up the bed of the Molopo. Into Mafeking he had got, but like many previous attacks had proved—it was easy to get in, but quite another matter to get out. The Baralongs and our outlying forts had allowed some three hundred men to enter, and had then commenced a heavy fire upon their supports. This discomfited the supports, and they incontinently fled. Silas Moleno and Lekoko, the Baralong leaders, had decided that it was better to kraal them up like cattle. One Dutchman was overheard to shout, "Mafeking is ours," when suddenly his friends yelled, "My God, we are surrounded."

This species of fighting particularly appeals to the Baralong. He is better than the Boer at the Boer's own game, and never will I hear a word against the Baralong. However, Silas was then engaged in conjunction with our own men in collecting them. He collected them where they had no water, and then the question resolved itself into the Boer showing himself and getting shot or gradually starving. If the Baralongs had been fighting the fight and time had been no particular object, they would probably still be shooting odd Boers, but it is obvious that those dilatory measures could not be pursued by ourselves, and that we had to finish the fight by nightfall.

Our men were accordingly sent down to round them up; there

were thus in all three parties of Boers in the town, one, nearly three hundred strong, in the B.S.A.P. fort, sundry in a *kraal* by Mr. Minchin's house, others again in the *kopje*. The *kraal* was captured in an exceedingly clever manner. Captain Fitzclarence and Captain Marsh worked up to the walls, but knowing the pleasant nature of the Boer, instead of storming the place or showing themselves, they bored loopholes with their bayonets. The artillery under Lieutenant Daniels also had come up to within forty yards.

There was a slight hesitation on the part of the Boers to surrender. The order was given to the gun to commence fire. The lanyard broke, but before a fresh start could be made the Boers hastily surrendered. Captain Marsh, known and respected by the Baralongs, had great difficulty in restraining them from finishing the fight their own way, and small blame to them for their desire. They had had their *stadt* burned. Odd Boers had been bolting at intervals, and had mostly been accounted for. The question next to be settled was as to the possession of the B.S.A.P. fort. Our men who were captive therein, and indeed the Boers and foreigners to whom I have since talked describe our fire as extraordinarily accurate. Eloff had great difficulty in keeping his men together, and as one man at least was a deserter of ours, it can't altogether be wondered that they did not wish to remain.

Our firing, as we had more men to spare, became more and more deadly, and at last now they decided to surrender. Some hundred broke away and escaped from the fort, in spite of Eloff firing on them, but their bodies have been coming in ever since and many will never be accounted for, because the bodies of men with rifles may be possibly put away by the Baralongs, who are always begging rifles we have been unable to give them. Eloff accordingly surrendered to Colonel Hore. The other party in the *kopje* had made several unsuccessful attempts to break out, Bentinck and his squadron always successfully heading them, but as it got dark, and our men had been fighting from before four, it was decided to let them break out and just shoot what we could. The Baralongs had some more shooting too.

As each successive batch of prisoners was marched into the town absolute silence was maintained by the Britishers, except saluting brave men who had tried and failed. They were brave men and I like them better now than I ever did; the *kaffirs*, however, hooted. As each batch marched up, their arms, of which they had naturally been deprived, were handed over to the cadets, who had been under fire all day. These warriors range from nine to fifteen years of age. They are

Captured Boer prisoners

the only smartly clad portion of the garrison, for our victorious troops were the dirtiest and most vilely robed lot of scarecrows I have ever seen, still it did one good to see the escort to the prisoners, they were simply swelling like turkey cocks and all round our long lines of defences we would hear cheers and "Rule Britannia" and the "Anthem" being sung with the wildest enthusiasm. It is impossible as I said before, to say who behaved best, but none behaved badly. There was only one thing said afterwards, when all sorts and conditions of men were shaking each other by the hand, and that was, "This is a great day for England." Mafeking is still rather mad with the Relief Column within shouting distance and it is likely to remain so.

We lost few men in our great success but I take it that no man particularly wants to be lost. I really have seen brave men here, but the man who says he wants to get shot is simply a liar. We know the story of the Roman sentinel and the Highlander who fought in Athlone (or was it Mullingar) against Hoche and many men that have died for their country obstinately. Captain Singleton's servant, Trooper Muttershek, may be added to their roll. He absolutely declined to surrender and fought on till killed. It wasn't a case of dashing in and dashing out and having your fun and a fight, it was a case of resolution to die sooner than throw down your arms, the wisdom may be questionable, the heroism undoubted. He wasn't taking any surrender.

As far as I am concerned, I have seen the British assert their superiority over foreigners before now, but this man in my opinion, though I didn't see him die, was the bravest man who fought on either side that day. It is a good thing to be an Englishman. These foreigners start too quick and finish quicker. They are good men, but we are better, and have proved so for several hundred years. I had always wanted to see the Englishman fight in a tight hole, and I know what he is worth now. He can outstay the other chap. Well, you must be getting rather bored by the fighting, and I will write more anon when I have collected some further particulars. The Rev. W. H. Weekes, our parson, organized a thanksgiving service on Sunday night. We were still rather mad, and it gave us a pleasant feeling to sing nice fighting psalms and hymns, because whichever way you look at it we are perfectly convinced out here that it is a righteous war. He had rather a mixed congregation, which probably in times of peace would be half the size, but he understands his congregation and the congregation understand him.

Poor Hazelrigg died that night.

Interviewing Boer prisoners on Mr. Weil's *stoep*

I went over and saw the prisoners this afternoon. They were very civil, and so were we. I like a Frenchman, and was chaffing them more or less at having left "*La Patrie.*" They didn't seem to mind being prisoners; they apparently enjoyed their fight, but they objected to their food. I did what I could for them, and I couldn't help feeling that they were absolutely uninvited guests. It wasn't their quarrel, and why they wanted to shove their nose into it we all fail to understand. There is really a very charming man amongst them, who asked me to procure him a grammar as he wished to improve his mind by learning Dutch and English. Of course, I got him a grammar, while I couldn't help suggesting that it might have been as well to remain in comfort in France without travelling all this way to learn the language, also remarking Dutch seemed rather out of date. He rather agreed with me, and asked me for a collection of siege stamps as he said he thought his girl would like them.

The funny part of these fellows is that they seem to think that we haven't got homes or girls or anything else, but are a sort of automatic "Aunt Sally," put up here for irresponsible foreigners to have a shy at. Nobody bears any malice about the fight, but the Frenchman calls the Boer "*canaille,*" the Boer doesn't seem to like the Frenchman or, indeed, any other foreigner, regarding him as an impetuous fool who would probably lead him (the Boer) into some nasty dangerous place, and the Englishman laughs at the lot; however, as I said before, the poor devils can't help being foreigners. I always like a Frenchman, a good many have been kind to me and they are invariably amusing. Their stomachs, however, are at present proud, and they cannot swallow "*sowen,*" or horse flesh, or any local luxuries.

However, as we pointed out, it was rather their fault that we had not any rations in here. Some of these men had only been in the country a week. It seems a long way to come to get put in "*quod,*" and live on horse flesh and "*sowens.*" One told me he passed a battery of our relieving column in harbour at Beira. I suppose he thought he had put in a smart day's work when he got ahead of it. He has, but he isn't working now. I never liked Eloff much, not that I knew him personally, but now I like him better for his performances. He very nearly did a big thing, but both sides have apparently an ineradicable mutual contempt for each other, which has led to some very pretty fighting through the whole war.

There is no mistake about it, he did insult the queen, and I am glad we have had the wiping out of that score, but he is a gallant fellow all the same. When we look back on our discomfiture of Cronje, and the mopping up of Eloff, it gives a pleasant finish to the siege. It wanted just a finishing touch to make it satisfactory. There should be another fight within a few hours, but I reckon that it will be the relief column's turn, and though everything is ready for us to assist them I honestly don't think we could go far and do much. The men were dog tired on Saturday, absolutely dog tired. I always thought the Boer was a bad bird to get up to the gun, but he came up that day. I don't think he will again.

On Monday we saw the tail end of some Boer force arriving. We had hoped it might be our own people, but they appear to be a few miles further off. However, we know they are there or thereabouts now. Nobody minds now, we know we are winning.

To return again to my story of the fighting, the foreigners did try their best to stop the Boers looting, but loot they did most thoroughly. They stole everything they could lay their hands on. Not one officer, whose kit happened to be in the fort has recovered anything. One "clumpy" of Boers galloped forth laden with food and drink. The food belonged to themselves, the drink belonged to us. They happened to fall in with the galloping Maxim, a piece of bad luck because they all died and our people took the food and drink. One fellow had taken a pair of brown boots and a horse, he had a few bullets through the boots, the horse was killed and so was he.

Life had been very dull here, but that morning put everything all right. We had never before seen a dead or wounded Boer or a prisoner, and it is weary work to see your friends and neighbours shot and not see your own bag too, but personally, except in the way of business, I hope I haven't killed a Boer. In the fight in the morning, though everything had been prepared for as far as we could tell, we had had to take up positions which were absolutely enfiladed by the fresh development of affairs. The trench occupied by the Bechuanaland Rifles, Protectorate Regiment, and others on the spur of the moment, was directly enfiladed by the enemy's quick-firer. Why we were not wiped out on that line I never shall quite make out.

They shot the jailor, Heale, who has done very good work all through the siege, who I am afraid leaves a wife and family. Then the prisoners took charge of themselves. Our gunner prisoners ran down to the guns, one was shot, the others served the gun all day. The others, armed with Martinis, commenced a heavy fire on the enemy, or cautioned the Dutch prisoners, the suspects, as to their behaviour, and put them down a hole. It was an exhilarating sight and struck me as exceedingly quaint to see men who had committed every crime, and were undergoing penal servitude, dismissing their past, oblivious of anything except the fact that we were all of the same crowd, and had got to keep the Dutchmen out. I hope Her Majesty will exercise her clemency; they certainly deserve to regain their rights as citizens.

We have had rather a dull day for some reason or other. A general idea pervaded the town that relief was at hand, and when towards evening a cloud of dust and troops were seen to the south-west, we most of us got on the roofs and looked at them with some interest. It transpired subsequently, however, that they were the enemy retiring before Mahon. They passed round the south of the town, and opposed him later.

16th, Wednesday. A dull day, but towards evening our relief was really seen. Everybody got on the roofs, and looked on at the Boers being shelled; most refreshing, but as they were not apparently coming in, people went to feed, and enthusiasm rather died away again, so much so that when Major Karri Davis, and some eight men of the I.L.I. marched in, he told one passer-by he was the advance guard relief force, the other only murmured "Oh, yes, I heard you were knocking about," and went to draw his rations, or whatever he was busily engaged in. However, when it became generally known the crowd assembled and began to cheer, and go mad again—so to bed.

17th, Thursday. Roused out this morning at some ungodly hour to be told they had arrived, and strolled down to the I.L.I. to see Captain Barnes of my old regiment. It appeared that Mahon and Plumer had effected a masterly junction the day before, and that the former, following the only true policy of South African warfare had, as usual, said he was going to do one thing, and done something else, *viz.,* camped out, and then suddenly inspanned and marched into the town. I can't quite convey the feelings of the townspeople, they were wild with delight, and pleased as they were their *bonne bouche* was to come later. Edwardes and Barnes breakfasted with me and then went back (personally I borrowed a horse from the I.L.I.). About 9 o'clock the guns moved out to the waterworks, and then the fun really began.

The Boers had been going to intercept Mahon's entry, but he was a bit too previous. All the morning their silly old five-pounder (locally known as "Gentle Annie") had been popping away, when suddenly the R.H.A. Canadian Artillery and pom-poms began, ably led by our

133

old popguns, who had the honour of beginning the ball. I rode well out, as I wanted to see the other people have a treat, but literally in half an hour all there was left of the laager, which has vexed our eyes and souls so much for long months, was a cloud of dust on the horizon, except food-stuffs, &c., which we looted. I got a Dutch Bible, and from its tidiness I was pleased to see its late owner was a proficient in the Sunday school. So, quietly back to the town, and after the march past of the relief column the relieved troops began. And now, I suppose, after being bottled up for some eight lunar months, I may effervesce.

As I have said before, I have seen many tributes to Her Majesty and joined in them all, but dirty men in shirt sleeves, and dirtier men in rags on scarecrows of horses touched me up most of all. We were dirty, we were ragged, but we were most unmistakably loyal, and we came from all parts of the world—Canadians, South Africans, Australians, Englishmen, Indians, and our Cape Boys and various other Africans, and there was not one of us who did not respect the other, and know we were for one job, the Queen and Empire, not one.

I wonder how the prisoners felt, poor devils; they must have wished they were not against us. The Boers had certainly executed the smartest movement I had seen for some time; I had not believed it possible that a laager could break up and disperse so rapidly. We all went back to lunch, having recovered Captain McLaren, who, I am glad to say, is doing very well. Then after lunch an alarm was raised that we had rounded up old Snyman, and everybody started off to help in the operation; but, alas, Snyman knows too much. They said that he and four hundred Boers were surrounded and refused to surrender, and we all wanted as much surrender as we could get—or the other thing.

I am glad to say he was hit on the head in the morning with a bit of shrapnel, but not dangerously wounded, unfortunately, at least so they report. He seems equally execrated by Dutch and English—Psalm-singing, sanctimonious murderer of women and children and his son takes after him. I may contradict my previous statements, but his actions have also varied frequently. Well, we had a great dinner; old friends from all parts of the world foregathered, and at our head was Smitheman. Many dinners then combined, and more old friends were met—so to bed, still pleased with England. Men of all sorts and conditions, trades, professions and ranks, relievers and relieved, slept that night in and about Mafeking, with a restless sleep, thinking of what England would think, and we knew and were sorry we couldn't hear

134

MARCH PAST OF THE RELIEVING FORCE.

what they said.

The garrison in Mafeking hope to get some recognition or decoration, but what they attach particular importance to is receiving the Queen's chocolate.

Immediately after the relief column marched in our Baralongs under Montsoia Wessels, Silas and Sekoko and Josiah, marched off on their own to settle up Abraham Ralinti at Rietfontein, and bring in our trusty ally, Saani. He had been utterly looted, and taken away from his own *stadt*, and kept a prisoner at Rietfontein, his great notion being that we should have a conference with the Boers, and then lay down what he called "plenty polomite," and blow them up when they came to confer. You cannot get very far ahead of a Baralong. I suppose this is the first occasion on which one black man surrendered under a white flag to another. These Rietfontein rebels have always been against the remainder of the Baralongs, and have invariably fought for the Boers since the disturbed relations between Briton and Boer have existed. I hope they will shoot Abraham, as his people's invariable cunning in stopping our runners has caused us great inconvenience, not to mention the numbers they have killed.

18th, Friday. Did very little. Went round and helped our pals to shop, get stamps, money, &c., &c.

19th, Saturday. The garrison held its solemn Thanksgiving Service at the cemetery, at the termination of which three volleys were fired over our dead. We had been unable to do this before owing to the certainty of drawing fire, not that that really much mattered, as they usually fired on all our funeral parties, though there could be no mistaking them. Still they had this excuse that the cemetery is fortified. After the last post had sounded we reformed and sang the National Anthem. Then, after Colonel Baden-Powell had spoken personally to each detachment, we cheered him, and then with heartfelt cheers for Her Majesty, the Siege of Mafeking closed.

GOD SAVE THE QUEEN.

And now for sheer personalities. Mr. Stuart had arrived, and as I considered he was much better qualified to represent the paper with the force than myself, I determined to come south. Mr. B. Weil, whom as I have previously said, I consider to be one of the principal factors in the successful defence, certainly as regards the food supply, said he was going south. I accordingly resolved to accompany him, and while returning from the ceremony suggested it. Anyhow, to make a long story short, I arrived as he was starting, and with a small bag, having relinquished all my Mafeking impedimenta, climbed into his cart. He had to turn out one of his boys, but I didn't mind that, and being the most good-natured of men, he tried to look as if he didn't. So our caravan started—Major Anderson, Major Davis (Surg. I.L.I.), Mr. Weil, and myself, together with his servant Mitchell, a prototype of "Binjamin," but absolutely reliable and hard-working, also Bradley, of Bradley's Hotel, Inspector Marsh, the Rev. —— Peart, and Ronny Moncrieffe (who had secured a horse belonging to a Protectorate regiment, and proposed to accompany us).

He had done a lot of good work in the siege, and was about as tired and unfit as a man could be. However, he was determined to get through, and so he did. It was a quaint pilgrimage, as the column, though it had swept the country, had not particularly cleared it, and the Boer is here today, gone tomorrow, and back the next day. Well, our commissariat was excellent. I contributed some eight biscuits and three tins of bully, and that is all I have done except live on the fat of the land—Lord, how fat it seemed after Mafeking—a land flowing with fresh milk, butter and eggs, mutton and white bread, and above all, the sense of freedom, I never knew what it felt like to be properly free before, and I have been more or less of a wanderer most of my life.

No more sieges for me, except perhaps from the outside. Yet I was sorry to leave Mafeking, and I may truly say as far as I know I didn't leave a bad friend behind me, only all my kit. Towards dark, after an outspan that was like a picnic, we reached Mr. Wright's farm, where the wounded were—one had died the night before—and we found Mr. Hands, *Daily Mail*, badly wounded in the thigh, but doing well; Captain Maxwell, I.S.C., and others. Mr. Wright acts up to his name. Two of his sons were in "*tronk*" at Zeerust for refusing to join the Boers, and what he had was at our disposal. I wonder if people at home realize in what a position our loyalists in Bechuanaland have been placed. If they didn't come in their own countrymen regarded them as rebels,—if they did they lost all they had.

But by doing as they have done, that is by carrying on their business while exposed to all the contumely and insult the Boers could heap on them, with the possible loss of life as well as property, they have served their country as well as those who have taken up arms;

because their houses have always been a safe place for runners to go to, and news about the doings of the Boers could be obtained from them. Besides, they know which of the Boers fought, and which didn't, and this fact now terrifies the rebels and keeps many quiet, who might not otherwise be so. Mr. Weil on arrival bought two hundred bags of mealies and despatched them to his friends the Baralongs. Such a pretty place his farm is, with plenty of water and lots of game.

We slept under the cart, and miserably cold it was. Mr. Weil (who is rather like myself in that respect), could not sleep, and was determined nobody else should do so. So we got up, and sat round the fire till sunrise. Our cocoa that morning was indeed acceptable. The caravan, which was as I say, quaint, marched as follows, preceded by mounted Kaffir Scouts:—First came Keeley and his boy in a Cape cart drawn by mules, followed by Weil, his servant, driver and myself in another Cape cart with six mules, Bradley driving a pair of horses in another, then Ronny, the Rev. —— Peart and Inspector Marsh riding, the latter riding B.P.'s brother's pony. We inspanned at sunrise on Monday and started for Setloguli. Halted half way and had the pleasing intelligence that a commando was raiding within six miles of us. I personally felt very unhappy. I had always looked upon it as a two-to-one chance, and as we had no weapons we could make no fight of it.

Apart from the bore of being a prisoner I knew I should be so awfully laughed at. However, there we were—it was no use grumbling, but I did, as hard as ever I could. Then we inspanned and drove to Setloguli, where our spirits were considerably raised by an excellent lunch provided by Mrs. Fraser, who is the best hostess I have ever met. The Frasers had a terrible rough time of it, and now "the Queen had got her own again" were naturally correspondingly cheerful. Later we were also further relieved to hear that "the commando" was merely a small patrol of Boers, and that it had withdrawn across the border.

During the afternoon I went up and saw the old fort—quite interesting, and anybody who wants to spend a quiet time might do worse than to go to Setloguli. The worst of it is it takes some time to get there. Lady Sarah Wilson's maid was there. She had been there since Lady Sarah was brought in by the Boers to Mafeking. Mr. Weil was showing various curios of the siege to Mrs. Fraser, including a copy of Her Majesty's *Leaves from the Journal of our Life in the Highlands*, which he had looted from the Boer *laager*. This excited the good lady's unqualified wrath, "What sacrilege for them to have it in their hands. Why it smells Boery," she said.

On Tuesday Keeley was returning to Mafeking with Lady Sarah's maid and his scouts, so Weil engaged two scouts to accompany us to Jan Modebi, where we were next going to stop. They didn't seem particularly pushing sort of scouts, as they persistently rode in rear of the Cape cart. The road too, was infamous, but it was impossible to lose the way as the column had left an unmistakable track behind them, and this was fortunate, because when we had been going about an hour and a half our intelligent guide stated he didn't know the way. I wonder how Keeley felt all that Tuesday. If he could have heard half we said he would have torn his two days' beard out and wept. The other scout lost us altogether. Keeley and Weil were arranging a series of despatch riders, so as long as we got one of them to Jan Modebi's, it didn't much matter. We outspanned first at a rebel's farm, and had an excellent lunch. I was still rather fretful. The prospect of captivity made me so, and I only believe in dead Dutchmen, till peace is proclaimed.

One Sonnenberg, a brother of some Bond member or other, was there trading, I suppose, like most Bondsmen, running with the hare and hunting with the hounds. He looked well on it, and was very civil. We inspanned and then came a long *trek* to Jan Modebi's. About halfway there, we saw two horsemen with guns cruising about. One obviously was not a soldier. I reckoned Pretoria was the ticket, however, they came up and Weil went to interview them. They turned out to be one of the Kimberley Light Horse and a civilian who was showing him the way, and he said he had got a convoy of cattle. It felt like being near home again then. We afterwards met the convoy—total, four white men and five black. I still marvel at their colossal impudence, marching through a rebel country within five miles of the enemy's border, escorting cattle for which any Boer will peril his skin. He calmly assured me they were going to pick up all they saw on the way; to use his own words, "All is fish that comes to our net." I hope they got through all right.

So to Mr. Menson's, where we put up for the night, and he, like everyone else, did all he could. He, too, had had a bad time. He didn't grumble, but when the relief column had come through they had cut all his barbed wire fences. Having a constitutional antipathy to barbed wire I sympathized with the relief column, but naturally did not say so. I was amused to see three prints of Sir Alfred Milner, Lord Roberts, and Oom Paul, the inscription under the latter being, "The end is better than the beginning, 14.10.99," also to hear his account of how when driving his cattle to Vryburg at the outbreak of the war he had met a Dutchman who told him that they had driven the English into the sea. His reply was, "Oh, that's too far to go," and so he turned and drove his cattle back again to his farm. Weil, as usual, bought up cattle, &c., also butter and other luxuries, and despatched them to the hospital at Mafeking on his own account.

Wednesday. We started rather later than usual owing to the heavy rain, and half way to Vryburg we crossed the fresh spoor of men, wagons, cattle, &c., going towards the Transvaal. It afterwards transpired it was the rebel Van Zyl and his following, bolting from Kuruman to the Transvaal. Let off number two. We couldn't have been more than an hour or two behind them, and they would certainly have scooped us had we met them, so the rain was lucky. Well, we got into Vryburg from one side as the troops got in from the other. An old acquaintance rushed me off to the Club, and I then strolled up to see the Scotch Yeomanry and found Charley Burn. I found also Kidd and several others I knew—then on to see Reade, who had been Intelligence Officer at Mafeking before the war, and was D.A.A.G. to General Barton, and arranged about getting on in the first train.

This was my first chance of seeing the infantry Tommy on the war path to any great extent. He is no more beautiful or clean, in fact, if anything less so than his cavalry brother, but by heaven he looks a useful one! However, what matter the man as long as the flag is clean. Met North of the Royal Fusiliers and dined with him, they all asked after Fitzclarence, Godley, and the others. They and the Scots Fusiliers had done quite an extraordinary march of forty-four miles in thirty-four hours, and now our infantry were within striking distance of Mafeking. The line should soon be repaired as they had begun from Mafeking and the line as far as Maribogo was practically untouched, in fact next morning, Thursday, they ran twelve miles north.

Thursday we began our preparations for departure. The garrison were preparing to celebrate the queen's birthday, and the populace to display great enthusiasm, and the women began to come into town. It was not a highly polished parade, so far as I could see. Still, it was rather good to have it there just then, where the Dutchmen had been in occupation within ten days. Rifles were now coming in by the hundred, and the rebel of a fortnight before became a British patriot. We drove to the station, and there met the Scots Fusiliers. I was accosted by a warrior in large blue goggles, who said I didn't remember him. I naturally didn't in the goggles, but it turned out to be Scudamore.

They did the best they could for us, and then Dick of the Royal Irish Fusiliers turned up, who had once been my sergeant-major. I was glad to see him—the old regiment and squadron seems fairly dotted all over Africa. Barnes was at Mafeking, three of us had been through the siege, and I met one Lambart at Taungs, who had been a corporal with us, and was a captain in the Kimberley Mounted Corps, curiously enough all belonging to two squadrons, B and D. Well, we left Vryburg with a light engine and a truck full of niggers. We were all sitting on the tank, in charge of young Gregg, R.E., who is a good train master. He ran us down, after dropping the niggers to repair a bridge, to Dry Hartz, where we had to pull out for an upcoming train, and as we had half an hour to wait, and it was just mid-day at twelve, we formed up and gave three cheers for the Queen and drank her health. It was the smallest and dirtiest Queen's Birthday parade I have ever attended; nine all told, but "*mony a little makes a muckle.*"

We ran down to Taungs, where one way and another we were detained some twelve hours. I didn't mind. The Royal Welsh Fusiliers were there, and I found several old friends and acquaintances—Gough Radcliffe, R.H., Cooper (Royal Fusiliers), Broke Wright, R.E., the former railway staff officer. So into a cattle truck we jumped with one of the Welsh Fusiliers and some men and arrived at Kimberley 7 o'clock next morning, where I called on Sir C. Parsons, and had fish for breakfast at the hotel. Thus my journey was practically ended. It transpired that Vryburg was held by some half dozen of our forces, and that the remainder of the garrison was only sixty loyalists from the town population.

It did not seem a large garrison, but apparently it was good enough. There was rather a curious coincidence at dinner at Orange River. I saw a man whose face I thought I knew, but I was mistaken; it was his likeness to his brother which misled me. He turned out to be Tom Greenfield's brother, who was down here sick, and to whom I had wired to meet me at Fourteen Streams, so that I could give him news of Tom. However, I struck him on the next river or so, so it didn't much matter.

It was sad to pass the Modder River and see our cemeteries—all English; so we passed on to Cape Town. And how jolly it was to see old friends; besides, we were able to tell our Mafeking people, womenfolk, good news of their husbands.

Three pleasant days there, and then everybody came to see us off by the *Norman*, which we nearly missed. The voyage passed without much incident. Everybody on board was more or less personally interested in the war, and there were a good many Boers and pro-Boers on board. On Saturday, short of Madeira, the *Briton* signalled the news of the fall of Pretoria. Tremendous rejoicings on board on the part of the British, while the Dutch were correspondingly depressed and seemed rather sad; some of them wept into the sea.

The further I got from the seat of war the less animus I felt. So to Madeira, where we arrived about midnight, and the news was confirmed with particulars. We got many newspapers. On to Southampton—more victories; many valuable officers killed. It is really sad to take up a newspaper; one sees friends killed in every fight. Thus we arrived in London at 9.15 on the 15th June, having left Mafeking 11 a.m. the 20th May.

"LORD NELSON."
By a curious coincidence the letters B.P. were found cast on the breech of this piece when dug up.

CAVALRYMAN

LEONAUR

ALSO FROM LEONAUR
AVAILABLE IN SOFTCOVER OR HARDCOVER WITH DUST JACKET

AT THEM WITH THE BAYONET *by Donald F. Featherstone*—The first Anglo-Sikh War 1845-1846.

STEPHEN CRANE'S BATTLES *by Stephen Crane*—Nine Decisive Battles Recounted by the Author of 'The Red Badge of Courage'.

THE GURKHA WAR *by H. T. Prinsep*—The Anglo-Nepalese Conflict in North East India 1814-1816.

FIRE & BLOOD *by G. R. Gleig*—The burning of Washington & the battle of New Orleans, 1814, through the eyes of a young British soldier.

SOUND ADVANCE! *by Joseph Anderson*—Experiences of an officer of HM 50th regiment in Australia, Burma & the Gwalior war.

THE CAMPAIGN OF THE INDUS *by Thomas Holdsworth*—Experiences of a British Officer of the 2nd (Queen's Royal) Regiment in the Campaign to Place Shah Shuja on the Throne of Afghanistan 1838 - 1840.

WITH THE MADRAS EUROPEAN REGIMENT IN BURMA *by John Butler*—The Experiences of an Officer of the Honourable East India Company's Army During the First Anglo-Burmese War 1824 - 1826.

IN ZULULAND WITH THE BRITISH ARMY *by Charles L. Norris-Newman*—The Anglo-Zulu war of 1879 through the first-hand experiences of a special correspondent.

BESIEGED IN LUCKNOW *by Martin Richard Gubbins*—The first Anglo-Sikh War 1845-1846.

A TIGER ON HORSEBACK *by L. March Phillips*—The Experiences of a Trooper & Officer of Rimington's Guides - The Tigers - during the Anglo-Boer war 1899 - 1902.

SEPOYS, SIEGE & STORM *by Charles John Griffiths*—The Experiences of a young officer of H.M.'s 61st Regiment at Ferozepore, Delhi ridge and at the fall of Delhi during the Indian mutiny 1857.

CAMPAIGNING IN ZULULAND *by W. E. Montague*—Experiences on campaign during the Zulu war of 1879 with the 94th Regiment.

THE STORY OF THE GUIDES *by G.J. Younghusband*—The Exploits of the Soldiers of the famous Indian Army Regiment from the northwest frontier 1847 - 1900.